Human Mind Power

The Power of Your Subconscious Mind

Jason Browne

from various sources. Please consult a licensed professional before attempting any techniques outlined in this book.

By reading this document, the reader agrees that under no circumstances is the author responsible for any losses, direct or indirect, that are incurred as a result of the use of the information contained within this document, including, but not limited to, errors, omissions, or inaccuracies.

Table of Contents

Introduction

According to Orison Swett Marden, whatever we aim at completing in life, we need to first bring to the attention of our subconscious, for without its approval, nothing can be done.

Are you continually searching for success but falling short of the mark?

Like most people, success is often measured by the accumulation of wealth, the size of your monthly paycheck, and the assets you own. However, genuine success is a great deal more than just the bottom line in your bank balance and what other people can see.

True Success Is More Than the Bottom Line

Why is it that so many successful people just seem to have it all: wealth, happiness, a successful business, a gorgeous partner, a flashy, fast car, and all the other trappings that go with their good fortune? Simply put, people with a positive, confident, and go-getting attitude are often among those who find the key to early success through harnessing the power of their subconscious. For these people, success encompasses every aspect of their life. You will seldom find a single truly successful person who is not victorious in all spheres of their life because they have developed the right attitude to accumulating wealth.

The subjective mind versus the objective mind

The subconscious or subjective mind gives your own personal meaning to all things that are seen, heard, and experienced through your senses and transferred to your conscious or objective mind.

An example of this may be as follows: You see a dog. I see the same dog. For both of us, a dog is an object that we can see, hear, and touch. Our conscious mind absorbs information via our senses about this object and categorizes it as an animal, or to be more specific, a domestic animal or a pet, or something unpleasant, potentially harmful or even dangerous to be avoided at all costs.

All this information is transported via a series of neurons from our objective brain to our subconscious. Here, our subjectivity takes control and decides whether the object we both see is actually what we believe it to be.

Your subconscious tells you the dog is a pet, and you automatically move toward it, feeling comfortable and confident about petting it.

My reaction is the opposite, as I view the dog as dangerous, and I have no intention of touching it. If fact, I choose to stay away from the dog.

Which of us is right in our subjective view of the dog?

To answer this question, we need to know about our backgrounds, our history with dogs. Your memories and experiences with dogs have been positive, fun-filled and caring. Mine has been unpleasant, fearful and painful.

Although our conscious minds have registered the objects we see as a dog, our subjective subconscious has interpreted the information differently. And, according to our individual subjective responses to the dog, we are in fact, both right according to our imprinted "dog-data."

The role of the subconscious in the accumulation of wealth and success

So, how does the analogy of the dog fit into our prospective plans for success in all areas of our lives, including our relationships, jobs, families, and social contacts, as well as our bank balance?

It's how we interpret what we see that brings us success. If we realize there's an opportunity for us to reach our goals, and we take it, we stand a better chance of becoming more successful than if we miss that opportunity.

As we have seen, depending on the historical data stored in our subconscious, we will react differently to opportunities that come our way. Some of us will view the opportunity as a fine chance to improve ourselves and grow our wealth. Others among us will see this chance as nothing more than a waste of time and effort.

The difference between the two points of view is the crux of what makes some people successful. Being able to spot a potentially lucrative opportunity and act on your intuition, you will ensure you have a better chance of success than the person who doesn't even notice the same potential niche in the market.

Our subconscious mind guards the gateway to our promise of success unless we decide to take matters into our own hands and push through that entrance with determination and enthusiasm.

The value of mind power

According to Richards, S., "You are essentially who you create yourself to be and all that occurs in your life is the result of your own making" (Richards, n.d).

According to John Kehoe, on a quantum physics level, we are all part of the universal energy field, and although each living thing vibrates at a different level, we are all interconnected.

When we send out our thoughts, we are in essence interacting with the "energy web of all reality," says Kehoe (Kehoe, n.d). Our thoughts are produced in our subconscious mind and are directly linked to all our memories and experiences. Hence, when we send out positive thoughts, the universal energy around us responds with positive vibrations.

Although this phenomenon may sound strange and unworldly to some, it is in fact based on science. The more control we have over our subconscious mind, the better our chances of success become.

Taking your thoughts for granted

Very few people ever take cognizance of their thoughts. If you were to ask someone what they are thinking, they may respond with a cursory answer, like "The girl sitting at the bust stop" or "The weather" or maybe "My wife, because she is ill." For the most part, though, these answers are superficial because they come from the conscious mind.

The thoughts we experience on a daily basis, including our fears and anxieties, short bursts of happiness, and sensations that we interpret as cold, hot, comfortable, or uncomfortable are seldom consciously noted. They are often overlooked as we rush through our daily routines, focused on the job, the meeting, tomorrow's plans for the kids, or the year-end vacation.

We miss many opportunities to take stock of our important thoughts and to use these to improve our lot in life. Our thoughts have the power to influence our lives, for better or for worse.

We attract what we focus on

Mindpower facilitates opportunities for us to focus on the things we desire (Kehoe, n.d).

If we focus on success, we attract successful opportunities in our lives. By making positive use of our thoughts, we encourage good things to happen. If you learn to use your thoughts wisely and well, you will soon realize the value of this power as you become more successful and happier.

This is, in essence, the Law of Attraction, which has been compared with gravity in that it is continuous, everlasting, and all-encompassing. Every good thought or deed goes out into the universe and multiplies. When you align yourself with this goodness and positivity, success comes your way.

If you desire something that you believe will improve your life, either on a social or emotional level, or, as is most often the case, on a financial level, you need to focus your attention on that desire to bring it into your reality.

Think for a moment on how people react to you when you are happy and excited. Their natural reaction is to smile and begin to feel happy too.

The Law of attraction works in much the same way. The more positive you are about achieving your goal, the more likely you will be successful.

Positive Thoughts Can Create a New Life

If you want to change your life for the better, start by changing your thoughts. Make these as positive as possible, which will train your subconscious to see the good in you and the potential in the world around you. Positive thoughts open your mind to endless possibilities for success (Kehoe, n.d).

Send out positive thoughts every day and make sure you request good fortune in a specific way. These thoughts may include your desire for a change in your job situation or a complete change in your career. They may include your dream of moving to another state or perhaps starting your own business. You may also be seeking that special someone to make your life complete.

Whatever you desire, frame this thought in a positive way and believe that it will come to fruition.

Don't give in to the temptation of your subconscious or to negative people who tell you you are wasting your time. Stay focused and positive.

True success can only be gauged by the number of times you are able to get up after being knocked down (Richards, n.d).

Our thoughts define us

Everything we think turns into actions or inaction. Sometimes, we react to positive or negative stimuli in a specific way based on how we understand the situation. Our thoughts, which are housed in our subconscious, create different scenarios, which we can take as Gospel truth, or we can question it.

Unfortunately, many people accept their thoughts without question, and the result is not always commensurate with the truth of the situation.

We are bombarded on a daily basis with a wide variety of information that we should sift through before we accept it into our conscious mind. This is, however, perhaps one of the most difficult things to do, because we are often victims of subliminal messaging received through advertising as well as through personal interaction with other people.

When we have the confidence to accept who we are, we become more comfortable to project our true selves to the world around us.

By being honest and true to yourself, you allow your thoughts to define you and thus, you become more competent in reaching your goals.

Repetition is the key

Consistent, positive thoughts lead to positive actions and, in turn, to positive outcomes.

So, by continually feeding your mind with good, positive ideas and plans for a happy future and a successful job, you create a kind of patterning cycle in your mind. Eventually, your subconscious imprints these positive pictures and ideas and begins to respond with more positive thoughts.

Gradually, you find yourself becoming more and more successful because you believe in yourself and have the power to control your subconscious into being subservient to only positive vibrations (Kehoe, n.d).

Mind Power helps you change your thought patterns

Your mind has the power to entice good and bad things with which it has a rapport (Richards, n.d).

When you learn to take control of your subconscious mind, you invariably begin to alter your thought processes. In turn, your thought patterns that have been in place for your lifetime begin to alter. Over time, these become more malleable and easier to replace with new positive ideas and plans.

By changing and upgrading your thought patterns, you begin to pave the way to your future success (Kehoe, n.d).

Make your subconscious your partner

You know now that your subconscious mind adapts and works on the thoughts produced by your conscious mind, so when you harness the power of your subconscious, you invariably empower yourself and begin to attract success.

Because your subconscious is like a fertile tract of land, what you plant there will grow and bloom. The more positive and uplifting information you store, the greater your success will be (Kehoe, n.d).

The converse is of course also true. So weed out the rubbish, the negatives, and naysayers to make room for the productive thoughts you need for success.

The importance of synchronicity

"The mind is a flexible mirror, adjust it, to see a better world" (Richards, n.d).

As soon as you realize the power your subconscious has to deliver what you desire, you will notice small signs of unexpected positive things that begin to come your way. Your energy synchronizes with that of the universe and begins to work for your benefit. Gradually, you will find yourself drawn to others of like mind and who will be beneficial to your ultimate success because each individual forms a small section of the entire unit (Kehoe, n.d).

Mostly, we are the masters of our own fate. We create everything that occurs in our own lives through our thoughts and actions. Be mindful of what you want to achieve and decide on how best to reach your dream.

A Bit About the Author

Why do we do the things that we do? Are we often acting on impulse, or is a certain powerful force propelling us into action? These are just two of the many questions that Jason Browne pondered in his teens and early adulthood.

Fascinated by the power of the human mind, Jason obtained his undergraduate Psychology degree from Stony Brook University. Later on, he returned to his alma mater and completed a graduate program as well as a doctorate program in Clinical Psychology.

In his work with clients, Jason has been focusing on the empowerment of others and showing them how they can regain control of their existence, their confidence, and even their mental processes. Through the years, he developed his unique, therapeutic methodology focused on the power of the subconscious mind and the strategies for reprogramming it.

Although *Human Mind Power* is Jason's first comprehensive book on the topic, he has written about subconscious mental processes for an array of specialized psychology publications.

Jason Browne lives and works in New York. He shares a beautiful, cozy apartment with his partners and the most patient Siamese cat you've ever heard of.

Chapter 1:

Consciousness Versus

Subconsciousness

The Nature of the Human Mind

The human mind is an amazing, intricate, complex, and complicated system that, despite continued scientific studies, is not yet fully understood.

The mind, which is the seat of our thoughts and all consciousness, is housed in the brain and consists of a number of vitally important facets. Each of these constituents or facilities is interconnected and interrelated with the others. Together, they operate the entire body and all its functions.

As an interactive, indefatigable physical and electrical entity, the mind is the powerhouse for all learning and actions. By its very nature, it is exposed to continuous information streaming into it, every second of the day, which requires processing and storage.

Since our birth, our mind has been in operation, absorbing through our five senses, all that we have learned through our continued interaction with our environment. This information, vital for our memories, our ability to communicate and think, as well as interact with other people on an emotional and social level, is vital for our successful existence.

The Cognitive Faculties of the Brain

Consciousness

Consciousness is perhaps the most challenging area of the human mind to understand. It enables us to be aware of, process, and understand both internal and external stimuli.

Our conscious mind identifies wakefulness. It is always in a state of "current awareness" and challenges us to think and respond to stimuli such as sensations, memories, feelings as well as fantasies, and all that we perceive through our senses.

For example, if you inadvertently touch a hot object, your brain registers pain and your mind immediately reciprocates by cataloging the sensation and how you responded to it. The memory is cataloged and stored for future reference, and you will remain wary of hot objects for the rest of your life.

Imagination

Our imagination is that part of our mind linked to our memory and that reproduces mental images either from past experiences or manufactures new ones through the use of your personal creative imaging skills.

Being afraid of the dark when you were young may have become a serious cause for fear. Your imagination may have run wild and led you to believe the worst possible scary "creatures" lay in wait to ambush you as soon as the lights went out.

Our imagination has the power to create fear and anxiety as well as pleasure and excitement from simple scenarios that it either fabricates from the evidence we already have stored in our mind or to recreate new scenarios.

Perception

Perception is the ability you have to identify, interpret, and organize the information received through your senses. Our sensory channels are the gateways via which information such as sound, visual images, smells, taste, and touch experiences enter our mind, bringing valuable learning opportunities about the environment around us.

For example, you are able to discern a variety of sounds around you and identify these and learn their specific purpose, as in the school bell from the church bell, your cell phone ring from the ringing of the doorbell.

Thinking

Thought processes are still an enigma to scientists as these are challenging to monitor and are highly personal and individualistic in nature.

Thinking involves our ability to allow our minds to consider many different possibilities on any number of subjects and scenarios. It gives us the opportunity to seek potential answers to specific questions and to resolve problems on a mental level.

For example, when faced with the dilemma of having to choose a suitable gift for your significant other, you will weigh up the available options against his or her likes, personality, interests, and the usefulness of the gift.

Judgment

Your judgment skills assist you in weighing up evidence and being able to reach a conclusion to make a decision that will impact positively on your safety, security, a long-term investment, or a special relationship.

For example, if you decide to invest in a well-known, successful company listed on the stock market, you may have made a sound judgment call with regard to earning a good return on your investment.

Language

Language is the complex system used for communication and is made up of verbal and non-verbal symbols and clues that we use to convey our ideas and thoughts in a constructive, organized manner, either verbally or in writing.

For example, when you want to demonstrate displeasure, your non-verbal communication clue might take the form of a scowl or a frown, while your verbal dissatisfaction will be encoded in words.

Memory

Your memory is that area in your brain that encodes and stores information in order for you to retrieve this when needed.

For example, as a child, you may have learned about road safety. Later in life, your automatic retrieval of that information will remind you of the rules of the road when you, for example, drive for the first time.

How We Perceive Our World

Perception relates to what we see, hear, taste, touch, and smell and how we understand these stimuli and relate to them.

Sensory stimuli are received in a number of ways:

What's that smell?

Aromas and odors are received through our olfactory receptors in our nasal cavity, and the information is processed in the olfactory bulb in our brain. It is here that the brain is able to establish the difference between good and bad smells.

Wow! That looks good!

The occipital lobe, located in the cerebral cortex, makes sense of all visual information collected from the optic nerve at the back of our eyeball. All the visual images are processed, cataloged, and stored for future reference. Visual information is also valuable in helping us to decipher non-verbal clues during communication.

Did you hear that?

Auditory stimuli are collected and processed in our temporal lobe, which is also located in the cerebral cortex. Here, we are able to differentiate between different sounds and words to understand verbal messages. The auditory information is stored in the form of songs, rhymes, words, phrases, and numerical patterns.

Yummy! That tastes good!

Receptors on our tongue, register specific tastes such as salty, sweet, bitter, and sour. This information is received, interpreted, and then stored in the gustatory cortex of our brain. This information will affect our food preferences and our positive or negative responses to certain smells.

Ouch! That hurt!

Our somatosensory system is responsible for the gathering, interpreting, and processing of all sensory stimuli received through our largest organ, the skin. Information is stored in the sensory cortex. It is here that the brain recalls the sensation of heat and burning, icy cold, wet, warmth, and pain.

The importance of how we perceive the world

Perception is the on-going process in which all our senses automatically collect a variety of data, which is then processed and accorded meaning in the brain. Every person interacts with their environment through their perceptual channels.

Sometimes, these channels supply stimuli and information with which we are already familiar, while at other times, the information collected is new and requires further cognitive processing.

Through our perceptual conduits, we learn about our world and develop our knowledge of how things work, ways to behave and interact with others, what things look like, and how they feel to the touch. We learn to enjoy certain foods and develop our taste preferences for specific items such as chocolate or salt.

The Three Levels of Awareness

The well-known psychoanalyst, Sigmund Freud believed that human behavior and personality developed from the interaction between three levels of awareness in the mind. These include the conscious, the preconscious (which is also known as the subconscious), and the unconscious mind (Cherry, 2019).

Freud's analogy of the human mind to a floating iceberg is perhaps still the best way in which to describe how the three levels of awareness interlink and function to create the total human experience as we understand it.

The conscious mind

The conscious mind, according to Freud's metaphor, is the visible part of the iceberg that accounts for approximately 10% of the brain's function. It is that area of the brain that includes all the cognitive faculties, including wakefulness or attention, memory, language, judgment, thinking, perception, and imagination. It is the seat of awareness and deliberate, rational thought, and reasoning.

All our feelings, thoughts, ideas, wishes, experiences, and memories are stored in the repository of our conscious mind, which is actively involved in all your current thoughts, emotions, sensations, and feelings. These cognitive faculties are used daily, and the information collected through your senses is processed, cataloged, and then stored for later retrieval. These channels are usually more easily recalled than those in the preconscious mind.

Our conscious mind is what molds us into the individual other people see. It's the space in our brain where we live, day in and day out, where commands are issued and processes are completed based on present information and actions.

Our conscious mind allows us to rationally process our thoughts, words, and deeds in a logical and sensible manner. It encourages us to communicate and interact with our environment through our senses, speech, writing, thoughts, and movement. Our conscious mind is, in fact, the control center of our lives.

For example, if you are currently studying mathematics, your conscious mind will recall the formula for the area of a circle when this information is required for your math exam.

Or you may be feeling tired, so your conscious mind registers this sensation and suggests you take a nap.

The Preconscious or Subconscious Mind

The subconscious or preconscious mind exists outside of our consciousness. It is that part of our mind that is "not currently in focal awareness" and is associated with impulses, feelings, thoughts, urges, and uncontrolled behavior patterns that exist outside of our conscious mind (Subconscious, 2020).

Your subconscious only operates under the direction of your conscious mind. It is unable to operate independently and thus cannot think or reason in isolation (Tracy, 2018).

The preconscious or subconscious mind is the area defined by Freud as existing between the conscious and unconscious minds. It houses all material in the form of thoughts, memories of sensory stimuli, reactions to stimuli, and feelings that lie just beneath the surface of your memory, hidden from 'view' until activated into full memory by a specific trigger.

The preconscious (subconscious) mind is comparable to a bridge that connects the conscious area of the mind with its unconscious section. Although all the information stored here is not currently in use, it is readily accessible when needed. It is not stored on the current memory disc, so to speak, but is relegated to a storage facility further into the recesses of your mind.

The value of memories

Memories in this huge "memory bank" in the preconscious mind are held in a state of limbo while they await a specific summons from the brain to enter the conscious mind. Once memories are recalled, you respond in a pre-programmed manner, based on previous experience to the same stimuli (Tracy, 2018).

For example, the smell of warm pancakes with maple syrup conjures a memory of early mornings from your childhood that has lain dormant until activated by smell. This thought is not always foremost in your mind but has been raised into your present awareness and consciousness simply by the correct trigger of the delicious smell.

All thoughts, memories, and ideas extracted from your subconscious mind encourage your behavior patterns to work in close conjunction with your hopes, fears, and desires.

Regulation of body functions

Your subconscious mind has a homeostatic impulse that regulates your body temperature and keeps all your body functions normally and in working order. These include regulating your autonomic nervous system that maintains your heartbeat and breathing rate, along with the essential balance of hormones and chemicals necessary for continued life (Tracy, 2018).

Maintain behavior

It also has the power to maintain your behavior so that this remains consistent with how you have acted and thought in the past. Your subconscious mind is the seat of all your memories, from birth until the present. It knows and recognizes what makes you happy or sad, what makes you comfortable or stressed. It elicits a sense of uncertainty and sometimes even fear when you are faced with the unknown or a stressful challenge for which you were ill-prepared (Tracy, 2018).

Habits are entrenched

The subconscious mind is also the source of your habits. These are so well entrenched in your psyche and are all but indelibly imprinted in your mind. Therefore, habits are hard to break or alter.

It is therefore essential that if you wish to break free from the ties of your subconscious mind, you should learn to practice positive reprogramming of your mind. Positive self-affirmation and pep-talks are an excellent beginning for re-aligning yourself with your goals. By unlocking the power of positive, and taking control of your subconscious mind, you will find yourself in a good position for achieving success.

Remember, the proverb "actions speak louder than words," so take immediate action if you want to succeed in life and realize your dreams.

The Freudian slip

Sometimes, we experience what is termed a Freudian slip when we say something unexpected and possibly unrelated to the current topic under discussion. The reason for this slip of the tongue, Freud believed, was due to information in the preconscious mind being triggered by a word, action, or perception of which we were not consciously aware.

The Unconscious Mind

Freud believed the unconscious mind made up approximately 90% of the human mind. All the unwanted memories, as well as the cognitive material the conscious mind wants to be suppressed, is stored away in the dungeons of our unconscious mind. Here, the information lies well-hidden where it is unlikely to surface unless encouraged to do so through the help of psychoanalysis or hypnosis.

Blocking the unconscious mind

Freud believed people develop their own personal blockade to their unconscious mind in an attempt to avoid having to confront any of the information stored within its depths. This barricade is erected via thoughts from the subconscious mind.

Although still a fairly controversial topic, our unconscious mind is considered by many psychologists and psychoanalysts to be a powerful tool that can be utilized for our personal growth and development, problem-solving opportunities, and the achievement of any goal we wish to pursue with good intentions.

Many of our fears, anxieties, feelings of inadequacy, bad dreams, and personal idiosyncrasies may be products of our unconscious mind and date back to our youth. When this information rises to the surface of our lives in the form of negative thoughts and behaviors, which is, unfortunately, the norm, it generally creates havoc and robs us of our reason and common sense.

Although we are unaware of the cognitive information in the form of feelings, memories, and thoughts that are stored in our unconscious mind, it is widely believed that auto-suggestion, hypnosis, affirmation, and the use of subliminal messages can be of value in controlling the power of the unconscious mind.

Which state of mind are you in when asleep?

During sleep, you are generally in a subconscious state, and the depth of this state will differ from person to person.

You dream, and it is believed that you experience deep-seated memories during sleep; however, much of what happens during these periods cannot be recalled when you awake. Scientifically, your brain activity can be monitored, measured, and clinically assessed, but when it comes to actually retrieve exact memories, this can only sometimes be accomplished through hypnosis.

Which is the dominant, your subconscious or your conscious mind?

Without a doubt, your subconscious mind wins hands down! It is, in fact, the archive of all that you have ever experienced in your life. Because it has been created or filled with information over a long period of time, it has vast areas of stored information that are challenging to access through your conscious mind.

However, the subconscious makes use of this information, sometimes using it to alter your perception of reality or to hold you back from pursuing your dreams.

The decisions made by your subconscious mind are often outdated because they are based on past experiences. The new situation you face may have similarities to previous experience, but it is unlikely to be identical. Therefore, the information you receive from your subconscious, which spurs you into acting in a specific manner, may not be entirely correct for the present situation.

Your conscious mind only reacts to concrete stimuli, things that you can smell, taste, and hear, as well as objects that you can see and touch. These are all things you will have learned to name and experience as you were growing up. Therefore, they all have a definite meaning for you, and you will react according to the information stored in your subconscious.

However, it is only by retrieving information from your subconscious that you are able to recall these experiences.

The subconscious mind is the mastermind for all you do say and think.

The Value of Neuroscience

Consciousness

Neuroscience includes the study of the cellular and neuro structure of the brain as well as its functions, and all its related systems, including the senses, problem-solving skills, and perception and how these relate to and affect human behavior, thought processes, and cognitive functions.

It also investigates the effects on people with disorders, such as those of a neurological or psychiatric type, and aims at furthering our understanding of the inter-relationship between the brain and the body to better address health issues that adversely affect these areas.

The results of these important studies may be of crucial benefit to delaying or possibly eradicating illnesses such as Alzheimer's and Parkinson's Disease.

Attention

Most people suffer from distractions and lack of focus during their day. These fluctuations in attention have been studied in an attempt to discover their source. Through the use of MRI scans, brain activity can be monitored.

Changes in attention have been linked to interruptions in networking in the brain. Although no conclusive evidence has been found, neuroscientists believe the constant exchange of information in the brain, involving the receiving, processing, cataloging, and responses, create a disrupted flow of electrical impulses, which may, in fact, be partly responsible for fluctuations in attention.

The impact of these studies on attention deficit disorder

Every activity and thought process requires concentration and focus. The implications of further studies into the workings of the brain with specific reference to mind wandering, its causes, and related outcomes may be of potential value to those individuals who suffer from attention deficit disorder (Sohn, 2019).

A number of informative books have been written on the subjects of neuroscience and attention.

The continued interest in the function of networking in the brain and its direct influence on attention, with specific reference to image orientation of small objects, is growing rapidly.

Research conducted in the 1990s by neuroscientist Melvyn Goodale involved people suffering from visual form agnosia. This is a condition in which individuals are unable to visually recognize and verbally indicate the form or orientation of an object, although they may pretend they can. However, when they reach for the object in question, their physical movements orientate to grasp the object correctly (Sohn, 2019).

The Important Takeaway Message

The human brain is an amazingly complicated organ that is the control center for all in-coming and out-going messages.

The conscious mind, which definitely occupies the minority seat in your mind, is the area in focal awareness where all current actions, thoughts, emotions, sensations, and feelings are experienced.

The unconscious mind is that part of your mind that processes information in an automatic fashion and to which you have no current access, such as your breathing, heart rate, metabolic processes, digestion, and the elimination of waste. It also plays a role in your balance, locomotion, and automatic responses to shock, fear, and pain. Your unconscious mind is neither available for self-examination nor open to your control.

The subconscious occupies the majority of your mind and is believed to be a vast, perhaps limitless storage area for all past experiences, thoughts, actions, feelings, and emotions and is the proponent for all your memories and responses to data collected via your conscious mind.

By bringing these three components of your psyche into alignment, you improve your chances of becoming a successful individual in any field of your choice.

Chapter 2:

The Role of the Amazing

Subconscious Mind

The Structure of the Human Brain

Our brain, consisting of a mass of "jelly-like tissue" contains over one hundred billion nerve cells called neurons. Each tiny neuron connects via a number of synapses with many others to create an interconnected network of electrical impulses in which thousands of new couplings are made every second of the day.

These connections are constantly modified as new information is received. This makes our brain the hub that governs and stores all our thought processes and memories, our beliefs, feelings and emotions, our actions and patterns of behavior, and all our life experiences. It is the epicenter in which all our learning and subsequent understanding take place.

The cerebrum

The exterior surface of the brain is constructed from a convoluted tissue and consists of the larger portion called the cerebrum and a smaller, anterior section called the cerebellum.

The cerebrum is divided into two halves called cerebral hemispheres. The left hemisphere is where our speech and language skills develop, while the right hemisphere is the seat of spatial awareness (Phillips, 2006).

The cerebrum is further divided into the posterior occipital lobe related to vision and visual perception and the parietal lobe, which is the seat of movement, the orientation of our body in space, and our ability to calculate.

The temporal lobes, situated behind the ears deal with sound, interpretation of speech, and auditory memory. The frontal lobes, situated to the fore of the cerebrum are highly developed in humans. This is where our complex thoughts, decision making, and planning skills are focused. They are also the seat of our working memory and are closely linked to morality, empathy, and feelings of regret (Phillips, 2006).

Below the cerebral hemispheres lies the cingulate cortex, which is responsible for directing our behavior and the level of pain we can accept. Under the cerebral hemispheres lies the corpus callosum, which joins the left and right hemispheres (Phillips, 2006).

The basal ganglia, also an important cerebral structure, is responsible for movement, motivation, and the desire for reward.

The more primitive regions of the brain

A number of regions, common to all mammals, lie beneath the frontal cortex. The limbic system is responsible for our urges and appetites. The amygdala, caudate nucleus, and putamen regulate our emotions, and the hippocampus is where new memories are formed. The hypothalamus works in close cooperation with the pituitary gland to regulate our bodily functions (Phillips, 2006).

The cerebellum, which is situated at the back of the brain is responsible for all our automatic movements, patterned movements, and repetitive tasks.

The midbrain, as well as the brain stem, control all our unconscious activities that are essential to life, such as breathing, heartbeat, blood pressure, and REM (Phillips, 2006).

The importance of genetics

Although the shape and structure of the human brain are partly dependent on the genetic code laid down by the parents, experience and exposure to learning opportunities also play a very important role in its optimum functioning.

Our brain experiences the prolific growth of brain cells during specific periods of our lifetime. This process, called neurogenesis, occurs during the first two to three years of our lives, again around the age of puberty, and culminates during young adulthood.

The impact of lifestyle on the development of the brain

As with all good health, the brain, like the rest of your body, is directly affected by what you eat and drink as well as by your exercise routines. A healthy body and mind place you in a prime position for positive learning and the successful achievement of your goals.

Despite continued research and studies into the brain and its functions, there is still a great deal of work to be done in discovering how the mind works. What defines us as humans have not yet been discovered.

Brain matter

Interestingly enough, the brain consists of grey matter, which is made up of the bodies of the individual neuron cells; the white matter, which consists of thread-like structures called dendrites; and glial cells which are believed to act as support cells for the neurons by increasing their neural activity when needed especially during mental calculations.

The role of the neurons

The neurons are responsible for the transportation of messages received through the sensory channels and then processed in the brain. This communication process is initiated and supported by a number of important chemicals, including dopamine, glutamate, serotonin, and endorphins.

Some of these neurochemicals assist the message-conveyancing process by collecting messages from release sites and moving them through the synapses to the receptors or collection sites. Other neurochemicals function in the brain tissue, either increasing or decreasing its sensitivity to stimuli.

These neuro-processes operate on a continuous basis throughout our lives. Any deviation from the neuro-program or deficiency in any of the chemicals leads to serious physical and mental challenges, such as Parkinson's disease.

A loss of serotonin can result in depression and mood swings. However, when the organic chemical, acetylcholine, decreases in the cerebral cortex, this may result in Alzheimer's disease (Phillips, 2006).

The Way in Which our Brain Activity is Monitored

The activity in our brains generates electrical impulses that can be monitored by an electroencephalogram (EEG). These impulses produce specific undulating patterns that indicate whether we are resting or actively processing thoughts.

If the pattern of these electrical impulses changes suddenly or dramatically, this may be an indication of a brain seizure.

There are a number of other methods used for monitoring brain activity. Among these are magnetic resonance imaging (MRI) and the diffusion tensor imaging (DTI). The MRI scan makes use of a large magnet and radio waves to study the structures in the brain. It is capable of identifying lesions and tumors. The DTI scan reflects the restricted diffusion of water in the brain tissue. Both types of scans produce computerized images of the results that can be used for further diagnosis and treatment planning.

The Functions of the Subconscious Mind

The mind and the brain are not one and the same, although the mind is a part of the brain. As noted in the previous chapter, the human brain comprises three important areas, namely the conscious mind, the preconscious or subconscious mind, and finally, the unconscious mind. Each of these areas of the mind has its own specific role to play, but together, they make up the most complex, intricate, and highly functional organ in the body.

To recap, your conscious mind is that area that collects and absorbs stimuli from your senses, interprets all this information, and forwards it to the subconscious mind where decisions are made for suitable responses and actions.

The subconscious mind is never at rest but constantly sorting, processing, and storing information for later retrieval. In fact, every action you make and subsequent reaction you go through starts in your subconscious mind.

The subconscious mind and our early years

It is strongly believed that good and unpleasant experiences from our youth have an impact on our current lives. This is due to the imprinted information received during childhood. For example, you may have been the victim of an abusive parent and although you may not publicly acknowledge your history, events, words, and the memory of specific actions are imported into your psyche and have become a part of your life.

Personal anxiety and fear could well be the result of an unpleasant experience suffered as a child. These memories may negatively affect your life in a number of ways. Relationships are difficult to sustain, holding down a job may be a challenge, or even simply demonstrating empathy and consideration to others may be difficult to do. This may develop into a social phobia that will negatively affect all your relationships.

The art of staying alive

You may now be aware of the huge importance your subconscious mind plays in keeping you alive. Why is this so?

Well, it's the part of your mind that is totally, and I mean TOTALLY in control of all the involuntary functions in your body.

These include your breathing, heartbeat, digestion, circulation, and all other involuntary processes that you don't even think about and which you take for granted.

Banking of a very different sort

What part of your psyche is touched by what you see, hear, and feel?

The subconscious mind is your very own personal storage facility of all your memories. Despite the fact that you may not immediately recall certain data, facts, experiences, songs, formulae from your college days, or details about your first car among millions of other snippets of information, they are all stored in the archives of your subconscious mind. Under hypnosis, some of this information is retrievable and can be used to assist you in dealing with fears, phobias, and anxiety issues that have their roots in your past experiences.

Have you ever wondered why you are sometimes drawn to a particular person, place, or object that you may never have encountered before? Your subconscious mind recalls data from as far back as your childhood, and on occasion, current events spark a familiar memory that creates a sensation of *déja Vu*. Your subconscious mind recognizes and then links the present event or incident with a past memory.

Absolute obedience

Your subconscious mind reacts only when given an instruction by the conscious mind. Once all the data collected through your senses from your interaction with your environment has been processed, understood, and responded to by your conscious mind, the memories and data are transported to your subconscious mind, where these are stored for the remainder of your lifetime.

Only when you require certain information will your subconscious mind give it up on command. The important thing to keep in mind is that everything you "feed" your mind is stored. So, you can create wonderful, positive, and productive storage or something negative and destructive.

Like the proverb says, "As you sow, so you will reap." If you continue to fill your mind with positive thoughts and self-affirmations, you are more likely to become a successful entrepreneur who achieves their goals (Galatians 6:7).

Maintaining the balance

Your subconscious mind is the great leveler in your life. It works in close conjunction with your autonomic nervous system to maintain your body's equilibrium, which is essential for the continuation of your life.

Without your subconscious mind's subjective actions of maintaining your breathing, heart rate, and body temperature, among many other important functions, the critical balance of your body would be upset, with disastrous results.

Your comfort zone

Because your subconscious mind is the seat of comfort and harmony, it responds immediately when you are faced with a challenging situation and attempts to restore order by forcing you to retreat to a more comfortable position. Any sort of imbalance creates a sense of distress that the subconscious mind fights to correct.

Successful people push the boundaries of their subconscious minds in an attempt to overcome the control that this part of their mind exerts on their potential success and creativity.

The importance of Mental Filtering

The subconscious mind has the ability to alter memories and information to change our perceptions. This filtering process, also called the selective memory process, is highly complex and develops over a long period of time.

In some instances, mental filtering can be viewed as a negative process that leaves you with distorted, incomplete, or otherwise curtailed memories. It may also have the power to increase negativity and depression.

In other instances, it may have some value in shielding you from excessive pain and allowing you to believe that you are coping with your life.

The main aim of the filtering technique is in its ability to either increase or decrease stress, alter your perspective on life and situations, or protect your mind from further trauma. This happens in a number of ways:

• Deletion of memory material

The subconscious mind has the power to delete stressful memories from its recollection storage facility. The power of the subconscious to delete offers us the opportunity to opt out, tune out, or omit areas of our experience. You may wonder why this would happen and even ponder its importance.

In instances in which you have suffered a horrific experience that has scarred your psyche for life, your subconscious mind may step in, so to speak, to protect your mind by choosing to delete information of this event from your memory. This action may prove beneficial to you in the long run.

However, sometimes, the subconscious decides to partially delete information, which distorts your memories, leaving you with an incomplete picture. This leads to confusion and a potential increase in anxiety as is the case with people who suffer from Alzheimer's disease.

• Distortion of cognitive matter

When the subconscious mind distorts information, this may have serious effects on the individual. Memories that have been altered are likely to lead to changes in behavior because the individual develops an unrealistic view of life situations.

In this instance, people begin to develop ideas about themselves and others that they believe to be true. Initially, these people present as very normal, often likable personalities who appear to be coping with life's challenges.

However, behind the scenes and deep in the recesses of their subconscious minds, they are uncomfortable with a specific scenario. Distortion allows us to alter perception or prejudice to view it differently.

Let's look at Sam, a father of two who has been married to Jane for 12 years. Their relationship has been fairly stable and could be judged as normal. Sam, however, has a needy personality due to having lived in foster care during the majority of his childhood. He is easily stressed by the fact that Jane appears to be becoming more successful in the corporate world than he is in his car sales business.

Sam begins to imagine Jane no longer finds him attractive and may, therefore, start looking elsewhere for a new partner. This leads to a distortion in Sam's thought processes in which he begins to believe Jane is having an affair.

Sam's distorted thought patterns will have a negative effect on his relationship with Jane with a potentially unpleasant outcome.

Distorted thinking results in unnecessary increased stress levels that lead to negative, adverse behavior.

- **Generalization of significant thought processes**

When the subconscious mind employs the technique of generalization, this may be a helpful filtering mechanism for learning important information. The mind sifts through vast amounts of stimuli, messages, and data, taking out only what it believes to be of importance to you in a specific scenario. In other words, the mind filters out everything it believes extraneous to the situation, allowing you to focus on the main points only.

This may work well if you only need to take cognizance of the important facts for your studies. Students who "spot" for exams, often employ this type of learning.

However, when your subconscious mind fails to present you with all the data, you are not sufficiently well informed to make a clear and significant judgment. So, when we make a generalized statement, we blanket an entire section of our experience with a single panacea for all ills.

For example, we may use a generalization for all homeless people being poor and potentially dangerous. Not only does this statement resonate with unforgivable prejudice, but it lumps all homeless people into a distorted and negative light without consideration of the many exceptions that exist.

Getting to Know Your Amazing Subconscious Mind

Your subconscious mind has the power to control your life and open the doors for wonderful opportunities for your success.

It challenges you to new heights and offers you the chance to realize your goals and become a successful entrepreneur in your own right.

However, in the words of Tim Ferriss, unless you keep it under control, your subconscious mind can become your "monkey mind" that begins to dominate and direct your thoughts and actions.

So, to take control of your subconscious mind, you should learn to communicate with it on a deeply emotional level. Unfortunately, emotions can have their roots in either negative or positive foundations. It goes without saying that you should avoid the negative and concentrate on positive thoughts and emotions to get the very best response from your subconscious mind.

Develop emotional intelligence

Emotional intelligence is the ability you can develop to recognize, control, and express your emotions in a positive and meaningful manner and that will help you maintain sound, well-founded relationships through empathy and understanding.

The more you develop your emotional intelligence, the better equipped you will be to interact with your subconscious mind.

Harnessing the power of your subconscious mind

There are a number of successful ways in which you can learn to harness the power of your subconscious mind, which include:

Avoid negative self-talk

The power our emotions wield over us is enormous and the most detrimental to our self-esteem and overall mental success is that of negative, degrading self-talk.

To regain your power over your subconscious mind, you should think, act, and teach positively about yourself. Think positive thoughts about who you are and recognize your worth. By practicing positivity every day, you will have the power to change your subconscious mind's picture of you, replacing it with a powerful, resourceful self, deserving of wealth and good fortune.

The retaliatory technique

This is a valuable technique for counteracting negative thoughts and words. As soon as you identify negative self-talk or some sort of self-degradation in the process, stop and turn your thoughts to the positive.

Commend yourself for what you have achieved and recognize all your good points instead of your character flaws, of which we all have many.

Each time you find yourself being besieged by negative thoughts and emotions, retaliate with plenty of positives!

Wipe out the negatives

You are ultimately in control over your subconscious mind, so when you find yourself thinking negative or degrading thoughts, press the STOP button. You are not obliged to fall into the negativity trap.

The Power of Desire

Desire is a powerful and manipulative emotion that can be turned to good or bad, depending on your plans for success.

When you exercise your power over your subconscious for good, your desire for success can outweigh any negative thoughts that may arise. This "burning desire" that drives some athletes and entrepreneurs is what can urge you too to achieve great success.

Consider Henry Ford, an industrialist and business magnate in the early 1900s, who followed his dream and eventually became the "founder of the Ford Company" (Henry Ford, 2020). He was driven by the power of his desire to reach the heights he did.

Ways to cultivate this desire

- *Set realistic goals*

Clearly and succinctly define your goal. Ensure these are realistic and attainable in the short and long term.

- *Destroy your safety net*

Destroy your safety backup and the "what if's" so that you can't retrace your steps, then set your mind in "survival mode" and step forward.

- *Accomplish small steps, one at a time*

Accept and accomplish to the best of your ability every small achievement and congratulate yourself on each achievement and use the positive energy this gives you as a boost to continue your journey.

- *Motivational triggers*

Discover what interests and motivates you, filling you with energy and inspiring you to want to achieve your goal and use this to keep you on track to the finish.

Develop Faith in Yourself

With faith, you can overcome most obstacles. Faith is a state of mind, an inner awareness of your strength and resilience that has the power to be translated into thoughts, then plans, and finally actions.

Physical preparation plan

Envisaging yourself as famous is one thing, but believing you have the power to achieve this goal is another. As soon as you visualize your goal, start making physical preparations to achieve it.

I believe that nothing worthwhile comes to those who sit around and wait. If you want success, feel the need, experience greed, and get moving to achieve!

So, buy that pair of skinny jeans and keep looking at them and seeing yourself in them as you begin to monitor your dietary intake. The more you see yourself wearing the jeans, the more motivated you will be to stick to the diet.

Broaden your options

Seldom do our dreams turn out exactly the way we wished them to. Remember that nothing is cast in stone. All your attempts to reach your goal will be fraught with challenges that may direct you in a different path. Ultimately, however, you will be successful and can look back on the road you traveled, marveling at the way in which you navigated the detours and stayed on track.

Communicating With Your Subconscious Mind

Communication between your conscious and unconscious minds is a continual two-way process. When you think of doing something, your conscious mind sends a message to your subconscious mind, which retrieves the information you require to complete the task. This process is almost instantaneous.

The threshold of conscious perception

The manner in which you address your subconscious mind through your conscious mind is what is called the "threshold of conscious perception." The faster and more positive your input, the better and more productive the outcome. The proverb, "he who hesitates is lost" is pertinent in this instance because if your timing is out or you hesitate, this could be the difference between noticing an opportunity and missing it completely (Mayer, 2018).

The power of auto-suggestion

Auto-suggestion is a powerful tool that we humans can utilize to control the input of messages into our subconscious mind.

Unfortunately, not everyone puts this power to good use. However, if you really desire something or want to achieve a specific goal, you can think and talk yourself into success.

The power of positive thought should never be underestimated as in the true story of Frances, who longed to open her own privately operated kindergarten. Despite the negative comments from her family, Francis remained focused and determined. She visualized the finished school building and herself at the door welcoming her new pupils. After a number of setbacks and with a few changes in the plan of action, Frances finally opened her school, and it soon became one of the best of its kind in the state.

Positive thoughts and positive, inspirational words lead to positive outcomes!

The Important Takeaway Message

Understanding that your physical brain is the single organ that maintains control over all the working parts in your body is important. However, it is not necessarily completely proven that the features of your conscious, subconscious, and unconscious mind are, in fact, embedded in specific areas in your brain.

It is, however, worth noting that without your brain functioning, the other three aspects will most certainly cease their processing capabilities.

Early identification of the value of your subconscious stands you in good stead to develop a deeper understanding of its worth to your success.

Understanding how your subconscious interacts with your conscious, hands-on mind provides insight into the interconnectivity between these two aspects of your mind, which gives you the opportunity to broaden your options for success by following the simple rules of engagement with your subconscious.

Being in control of your subconscious allows you to decide what information will be filtered, deleted, or altered.

Chapter 3:

Developing the Power to Control Your Subconscious Mind

Do you have the power to control your subconscious mind? Indeed, you do. However, this power has to be learned and practiced if it is to be successful.

For those of us who have supremacy over our subconscious minds, we hold the power of the world in our hands. However, this control does not develop overnight.

The subconscious mind, as we have seen, is the most powerful part of our brain, into the resources of which, we can tap at any time. If we fail to take control over our subconscious mind, it will, in all likelihood, exercise control over us.

Learning to control your subconscious is a challenging task as it has had years of practice and you are now new at this game.

Understanding Your Subconscious Mind

The subconscious mind is like a fertile field in which you plant the seeds of all your ideas, thoughts, memories, feelings, and emotions. Here, they grow and flourish or wither and die, depending on the care and attention you give them, says Richard J. ONeill (ONeill, 2018).

If, therefore, you realize you are the creator of all your subconscious holds, you will make every effort to ensure there's lots of good stuff stored.

Unfortunately, sometimes, bad things happen in our lives, over which we have no control. And although these unhappy and perhaps frightening memories cannot be undone, we can work hard to recall them and find something positive that may have occurred because of them. In this way, we repeatedly remind ourselves of the good and positive things in life. Eventually, these happy, positive thoughts will replace our negative ones. The magnificence of the human mind lies in the fact that it is the most complex organ in the human body that is made up of three distinct parts and a multitude of sub-sections.

As much as we may have believed our conscious mind is in control of our lives, we are very much mistaken. The subconscious mind, although apparently dormant for the most part, is, in fact, the conductor and orchestrator of all our thoughts and actions.

The subconscious mind is where the controls are kept for all our bodily functions, such as our breathing, heartbeat, and body temperature. It also maintains control over the millions of chemicals that are necessary for a healthy life and harmonious living.

The power of the subconscious mind rests in its innate ability to run your life, from your emotional level to your intellectual status and from balancing your physical self to taking control of your mental self.

By monitoring incoming messages from your senses, the subconscious also acts as an early warning system by reacting to negative stimuli that could cause you harm.

Your subconscious absorbs all the information you learn through your interactions with your environment. It sorts and stores this information, categorizing each little scrap of data according to previous similar information.

Now, based on your subconscious mind's interpretation of the data it receives, it develops the ability to control all aspects of your life by mimicking previous information and repeatedly bringing it to your attention.

Once you realize and understand the power of your subconscious mind, you will be able to utilize this potent energy to your good.

Learning to Control Your Subconscious Mind

Step one - Understand the subconscious mind's purpose

By learning to interpret the intentions of your subconscious mind, you will be able to take control of its thoughts and redirect its instructions for action.

Generally, the subconscious mind overrides the conscious mind, which has no real ability to think for itself. Because the conscious mind is intent on gathering, processing, and storing information, it relies on the subconscious mind for instituting all actions and responses.

Once you understand this process, you can begin to take control of your thoughts and decide how best to plan the required action from your subconscious mind.

At first, your subconscious mind may appear like a willful child, hell-bent on self-destruction, but with care and consistent handling, you can win it over to your point of view.

Step two - Speak positive, kind words to yourself

Speak kindly to yourself. Praise your efforts and remind yourself of the proverb, that although Rome wasn't built in a day, it became the mighty powerful capital city in Italy, over a period of time (Wiest, 2018).

Avoid negative emotions and words as these have the tendency to spiral out of control, allowing your subconscious mind to develop the power to curtail any positive energy and the prospect of a successful conclusion to an otherwise simple scenario.

The countering technique

Every time a negative thought arises, counter it with a positive thought. In this way, you challenge your subconscious mind to a duel in which the positive thoughts and words should win the day.

Each time you speak positive words about yourself, these are recorded in your subconscious until they become your way of life. If you tell yourself you are a reliable, hard-working person with a great sense of humor and the potential to go far in life, you begin to walk your talk and live up to your vision. Over time, others will begin to see you as the successful, enthusiastic go-getter that you have become. They will want to identify with you and emulate your ideals in the hope that they too will become successful.

Step three - Positive, uplifting thoughts

At the same time you are speaking kindly to yourself, you will be filling your brain and mind with uplifting, positive thoughts that point to success. By thinking positive thoughts and dreaming about success, you are already more than halfway to winning the battle (Wiest, 2018).

The subconscious mind is all too often programmed with negative thoughts and fears of "what if…" or "I'm not sure I'm up for the challenge!"

By turning a deaf ear to these naysaying comments, you take the lead and your subconscious mind will learn to be obedient.

Step four - Positive, well-planned actions

Fill your life with positive, well-planned actions that lead you toward your final, successful destination.

Don't dither or procrastinate along the way. Remain focused and mentally in tune with your plan, and your subconscious will not be able to shake you from your goal (Wiest, 2018).

Step five - Allow yourself to expect change

Any form of control changes things around you. So, if you decide to take control of your subconscious mind, you must expect to see some changes, for the better, in yourself. Look forward to your growth and development with enthusiasm and without prejudice.

Step six - Give yourself permission to aim for success

Change your mantra to one of positive self-affirmation in which you tell yourself daily, "I deserve success, happiness, and peace." Don't see your success in terms of "If I lose some weight, I'll be happy," or "If I can just get that big order, my business will flourish and then I will be successful" (Wiest, 2018).

Be happy with what you have and know that success will come to you if you really desire it with all your heart and mind.

Step seven - Avoid other people's doubt

Stay away from negative people who may want to "rain on your parade" by ruining your dreams with their pessimistic outlook on life and their cynical comments.

Sometimes, these people fear the outcome of your adventure because they are not sufficiently courageous to take action of their own.

By dis-allowing them to rob you of your opportunity for success, you empower yourself for the journey.

Step eight - Surround yourself with a positive, supportive entourage

Build small items of success into your daily life and keep company with like-minded people who will motivate you and cheer you on.

Buy yourself flowers or a bottle of champagne. Place inspirational messages in strategic places in your home and office and read these every day (Wiest, 2018).

Walk with a bounce in your step and feel positive.

Follow other people who are successful and take a leaf out of their book.

Involve yourself with other positive, like-minded people with visions of their own.

Step nine - Speak your success to yourself and others

Remind yourself and others that you are on the road to success. Change the way you talk about your goals. Try to remain positive and focused and tell yourself you are happy and deserving.

Positive affirmation is a great way to build self-esteem and confidence.

Step ten - Create a visual "vision area"

Having ideas of what you want to achieve is admirable, but sometimes adding visual material and positive words and phrases can give you the edge.

Create a special vision board in an easily accessible spot in your home or office on which you place pictures and uplifting words and phrases of your dream and what you want to achieve. This "vision area" brings your ideas to life, and by seeing them daily, your enthusiasm continues to grow (Wiest, 2018).

Step eleven - Identify your opposition

Many times when you feel excited about a new idea, "damp squib" thoughts douse your enthusiasm.

Identify the thoughts and feelings that hold you back and decide if these are, in fact, valid reasons to postpone your journey (Wiest, 2018).

In most instances, these thoughts are based on fears of rejection or failure. For example, "What will my friends and family say if I fail?"

Re-think those thoughts in terms of your success and how proud people will be of you. Have faith in yourself, and others will begin to have faith in you as well.

Step twelve - Ensure you have developed a master plan for your life

Although planning is essential for life to run smoothly, there is no way of knowing what waits just out of sight.

Long-term plans can go awry because change occurs unexpectedly from time to time. So, rather prepare an overall, master plan for your life, include where you want to be when you reach 50, what job you will be doing then, how much money you wish to earn, where you want to live, what car you will be driving, and more (Wiest, 2018).

Then, set out to achieve your plan. There is no time limit, so just focus on the end goal and continue to strive toward it.

Step thirteen - Keep a gratitude journal

Gratitude is a virtue you should hold close to your heart. Being grateful for everything in your life, no matter how insignificant the thing may appear, is the starting point for achieving your goals.

Showing gratitude for where you are right now makes you humble and ready to face the future with hope in your heart.

Once you are grateful for what you have, you open yourself to receiving more, while those who covet what others have achieved through hard work and effort remain miserable because they never believe they have enough (Wiest, 2018).

Step fourteen - Ask and you shall receive

Don't be afraid to send your requests out into the universe. When you ask with an honest and humble heart, you are more likely to receive in abundance.

Sometimes, we fail to step forward to ask for that raise which we know we deserve, or to invite that attractive brunette out to dinner. As the old proverb goes, "He who hesitates is lost."

Don't waste the moment. Go out there and at least ask. What's the worst that can happen? You are turned down. So what? Go back out there and try again!

Step fifteen - Learn to problem solve

There are many ways of reaching your goal. Perhaps the way you have chosen is fraught with challenges, such as insufficient production of goods or delivery problems.

Take stock of the situation and decide on a different way to solve the problem. Maybe you need to employ another person to assist you, or perhaps you need to reschedule deliveries to make the route you travel easier and more economical.

Problem-solving is part of your success. And remember, nothing comes easy without effort.

How Does Your Subconscious Mind Work?

Your subconscious is the section of your mind that you are not actually aware of. It is the storage facility for all your emotions, feelings, beliefs, life experiences, and memories.

It is the creator and arbitrator of your behavior and personality. It dictates how you will feel and react in certain situations when your emotions run high. So, if you are afraid, your subconscious mind will either encourage you to run away or to stand and fight.

It has the power to issue false information about you and other people as well as to fabricate about a situation and to bend the rules. This is why, so often at the scene of a motor vehicle accident, no two eye witness accounts match. Each person is led by their own subconscious mind's interpretation of the scene.

Working with your subconscious mind

Your subconscious mind is already programmed with beliefs about you and others that were laid in your psyche as you were growing up. Gradually, over time, you unconsciously believe yourself to be worthless or useless or a failure because of the information that has been listed in your memory bank.

Un-program the memory facility

To un-program, this storage facility will take a great deal of time and effort because all the information there is what the subconscious mind continues to use as its point of reference.

So, just talking positively and behaving in a dynamic manner will not change the mindset of your subconscious. Like any memory storage device, you will have to delete certain information to make space to store new facts and data.

So too, with your subconscious mind. You will need to reprogram, over-ride, or delete certain information to change your subconscious data framework to view you in a more positive light.

Act positively all the time

Continuous, repetitive, positive actions will eventually reprogram your subconscious mind if these are sensible and understood as being realistic and attainable.

The subconscious mind is way too smart to be coerced into believing fairy tales, so stick to the truth and reality when you set your goals for success.

There's No Magic Involved

The subconscious mind acts on facts and visible, tangible data received through the sensory channels via the conscious mind. It can only work with what it has and is incapable of providing magical solutions to your problems.

Through learning to know and understand your subconscious mind, you will realize the value of working in tandem for the ultimate, overall good of yourself.

The Important Takeaway Message

Understanding the authority your subconscious wields in your life enables you to learn valuable skills to control this power for your own ends.

The most important aspect to consider when considering exercising control over your subconscious is to first understand why you are automatically motivated to behave the way you do in specific situations.

For example, if you blow a fuse when someone takes your parking space despite being calm before this event, try to rationalize where this anger erupted from. Make a conscious decision to filter out this negative emotion, if not before you explode, then soon after.

The filtering scenario may take the form of asking yourself why this was your involuntary course of action. Perhaps you recall a distant memory of your parents behaving in a similar fashion. Try also to recall how you felt during this angry episode. Now realize those around you are experiencing the same shock, fear, and dismay.

Get in touch with that memory and make a concentrated decision to replace the outcome with a more positive scenario.

Consistent interaction between your conscious and subconscious minds is of paramount importance to your overall success in achieving your goals. By strengthening this connection, you will have the power to un-program certain memory facilities in your subconscious and replace these with positive, uplifting messages and memories that will work in your favor.

Chapter 4:

Strategies to Reprogram

Your Subconscious Mind

According to Earl Nightingale, all the information we store in our subconscious mind via repetitive input through our senses and our emotions will eventually become our own truth (Ziogas, 2019).

Your subconscious mind, as you have already learned, is the powerful controller of your entire life. From your food preferences and the way you interact with other people to your understanding of reality and your emotional response to an event, all your thoughts, actions, and responses and emotions are under the control of your subconscious mind.

The Value of Reprogramming Your Subconscious

Because your subconscious mind is manipulative and more often than not coerces you into thinking, believing, and behaving in a specific manner, you may have been forced into considering yourself a failure.

So, sometimes, when you have a great idea you decide not to carry it through for fear of failure. Your subconscious mind has robbed you of your confidence and the opportunity to prove to yourself and others your capabilities.

Once you realize your subconscious mind has sabotaged your chances of pursuing an exciting opportunity, you may decide enough is enough and make a stand by reprogramming this controlling mechanism to suit your dreams of success.

As soon as you make this decision, daunting though it may be at first, you begin to engage in an interactive partnership with your subconscious in which you take up the reigns of leadership and control.

Science tells us that the brain has the ability to develop new neural pathways through the process of neuroplasticity. This has been of huge value for accident victims who have been able to re-learn new skills.

During our lifetime, neuroplasticity plays an important role in facilitating learning for us as well as in the development of new thoughts, actions, and emotions, which are often of a negative genre.

We are exposed to a greater variety of negative scenarios in life that lay themselves into our subconscious and that eventually become part of our daily thinking and in some cases, our expectations.

Once we become aware of these negative vibes, we have the opportunity to change them for something more positive. By practicing more productive thoughts, we have the ability to reprogram our subconscious and bring it into line with a happier, kinder, and calmer existence.

Your subconscious is like a sponge

Because your subconscious mind is like a huge sponge, soaking up every tiny scrap of information fed to it via your conscious mind, it has become a reservoir for all your experiences and learning.

During your childhood, your subconscious accepted as Gospel truth everything it learned because there was no prior frame of reference against which it could compare the information it received. So, if you were verbally, emotionally, or physically abused during your early years, that information was laid down as the blueprint on which you based all future understanding of relationships, as well as your self-image.

Your subconscious is your auto-pilot

Your subconscious mind is similar to the auto-pilot on a plane. Once programmed, the auto-pilot will fly the plane along the set path toward its destination, without human interference. The only time that flightpath can change will be when the pilot re-programs the computer or forcefully takes the controls to guide the plane manually.

The only way in which you can change or reprogram your subconscious mind is through repetitive input of specific information that will eventually be paid back to you through the realization of your goals.

To alter the foundation of the knowledge held in your subconscious mind, you will need to replace the "old circuit board" with a newer, upgraded digital model.

Challenging the power of your subconscious mind

So, if you believe you are too stupid to do the math because earlier in your life, a teacher told you you were wasting your time because you just didn't have what it takes to understand the subject, the chances are you either dropped math at the first opportunity or you keep reminding yourself you can't cope with anything requiring numerical computations. The impact this has on your life could be that you avoid any future jobs or tasks involving math. You won't even consider training to become an accountant, a teacher, a doctor, or a pilot. What a waste, when you could become anything you wish to be, with the right attitude and approach.

The Reprogramming Plan

The most important aspect to consider here is once you have decided to reprogram your subconscious mind, stick with your strategy of choice. You will require remaining focused and determined if you are to succeed at overwriting the existing operating program in your subconscious mind.

You also need to develop a stoic attitude toward the process that will not allow you to give up half-way through the task.

Your subconscious operates out of emotion

Although meditation can help you to off-load some of your negative emotional baggage, it may not cope with the years of stored thoughts and emotions you have locked away in your subconscious. You may have become a victim of these pent-up, angry, destructive thoughts that appear to be ruling your life.

Your subconscious operates more on an emotional level than any other and is therefore easier to access via the emotional channel. If you consider any of the serious obstacles you have had to face in life that have had a devastating effect on your psyche and which have left you with deep-seated anger or emotional hurt, you may benefit from practicing some of the methods mentioned below to reach solace and understanding.

Steps to Reprogramming Your Subconscious Mind

Tony Robbins' Priming Method

According to Tony Robbins, all the emotions we experience is as a result of movement and action. He suggests that by changing your physical state of movement, you will change how you feel about the challenge you may be facing.

He recommends the following advice to get started:

- Find a comfortable area where you can sit with your eyes closed and your hands raised.

- Breathe deeply through your nose for 90 breaths, done in a set of 30 at a time.

- On each breath, make your hands into fits and push your arms forcibly downward as if you were doing a bench press.

- Once your breathing session is complete, sit quietly and feel gratitude and self-love and appreciation.

- Your mind should be relaxed and your body and brain filled with life-giving oxygen, which will promote the development of healthy happier thoughts and the opportunity to think more clearly and objectively (Pietrzak, 2019).

The Demartini Method

Dr. John Demartini, a human behavior specialist, makes use of neuroplasticity to reformulate thought patterns in the brain. He uses a question and answer method to help clients replace negative thoughts with more positive, interactive ones.

A number of important structures in the brain, namely the hypothalamus and amygdala, which control our expressions of fear, guilt, and aggression, are altered to alleviate the negative emotions and create a sense of well-being.

By questioning the source of your guilt, anger or fear, you are often able to pinpoint the reason for the negative emotion you are experiencing. With this knowledge, you can tackle the problem out in the open, so to speak, and find a lasting solution.

Perhaps you lost your job due to the jealousy of a colleague who lied about your integrity. This has left you with deep-seated impotent anger because you are unable to find any recourse for your ill-treatment. By understanding the source of the violent emotion you experience, you can begin to replace the negative thoughts with positives one about yourself (Pietrzak, 2019).

Tony Robbins' Affirmations

It is very easy to fall into the routine of our daily life and continue to do the stuff we have always done, because this requires no effort. The longer we stay in this rut, the deeper our negative neural pathways become.

Using positive affirmations on a daily basis that lift our emotions and help to create a positive aura in which we can move and work throughout the day effectively reprogram the neural pathways in our subconscious.

Use consistent, positive affirmations to reprogram the old material in your subconscious mind. It's easy to absorb negative images, messages, advertisements, and interactions because we are surrounded by these every day. We hear and watch bad news, witness aggression and anger between people, and we are caught up in the daily grind from 9 to 5 week after week.

The challenge is to stay positive through the mayhem and fill your thoughts and speech with positive affirmations. These can be about yourself, your family, and other people. When we use kind, positive words, we often employ empathy, which is a positive emotion.

If your affirmations are directed only at yourself, replace all the negative thoughts and beliefs with positive, uplifting ideas. Tell yourself that you are wonderful, unique, and capable of achieving great things, and BELIEVE this is possible. It's no good just paying lip service.

Affirmations help to create new, positive ruts in our subconscious. They lay the foundations for "new operating instructions" in your mind that become like that favorite song you hum frequently throughout your day. These, in turn, begin to override the negativity with a layer of positive good thoughts and emotions. Over time, the positives take hold and become our ways of life, our pattern for living. Ultimately, we begin to feel happier, more at peace with the world. We begin to experience success, perhaps in small ways to begin with, but as we acknowledge these successes, we allow for more to come our way (Pietrzak, 2019).

Using positive affirmations on a daily basis helps to create a positive aura in which we can move and work throughout the day.

Learn to be humble

Your subconscious mind has been with you from birth and it is, in fact, the sum total of all you have learned and experienced since then. IIt knows more about you than you do and understands your shortcomings and strengths.

Learn to listen and acknowledge your subconscious mind's wisdom, without falling victim to its manipulative plan.

Confusing as this may sound, take the following scenario as an example. Ben was a great swimmer who envisaged the sport as his life's goal, despite the fact that his subconscious kept nudging him to find a more consistent source of income.

Ben developed a high opinion of himself as he progressed from winning the swimming championships at school, then college, and was finally invited to join the national league.

He felt he was totally in control of his life, and he turned a deaf ear to the murmurings from his subconscious. Sadly, after an auto accident, Ben's swimming career came to an abrupt halt.

When his subconscious stepped in with "I told you so," Ben realized he needed another goal, and a lucrative one at best. He began to plan around his love of the sport and reprogram his subconscious mind to believe that his dream was still possible. In spite of the opposition from family and friends, Ben opened a swimming training academy and has never looked back.

Environmental stimuli

As you participate in your daily routines and life experiences, your subconscious mind is continually absorbing information.

If the environment in which you operate is filled with negativity and stress, your subconscious mind will absorb all these stimuli and make them part of your frame of reference.

Stop for a moment to take cognizance of the place in which you live, work, and operate in your life routines.

Reduce your exposure to negativity in every form, be this in the form of toxic friends or work environment to depressing news broadcasts on television and the type of literature you read. Change your environment to a place of harmony, filled with the sorts of things that will bring you peace and satisfaction.

Acknowledge and face your fears

Fears are negative feelings and sensations that lurk in the back of our mind, warning us of untold disasters if we step into the unknown.

Everyone has fears of one kind or another. When you have the courage to acknowledge the source of your anxiety and fear, you take the first step toward combating that fear.

By listening to what makes you fearful and anxious, you are able to make decisions to conquer your fear thus freeing yourself to follow your goal.

The power of visualization

"What you imagine, you create." —Buddha

 The power of visualization lies in its ability to help us refurbish our neural pathways by bombarding them with plenty of positive thoughts, mental pictures, and good feelings.

By creating vivid, detailed images in your mind of what you want to achieve, you attract positivity into your life and open your mind to the endless possibilities for success.

Your images can be of a dream job or home, of a special relationship, or something more material such as a fat bank balance.

By envisioning these mental pictures in a calm yet positive manner, you will begin to attract healthy calm vibes. As you think, so you manifest. If you are angry and upset, you display those feelings through your actions and words. By altering your state of mind, you immediately change your actions.

To develop the "emotional resilience" you require to make positive progress in life, you should begin to practice visualization on a daily basis (Pietrzak, 2019).

Through your inner faith, you have the power to visualize your end goal, complete and with you in control. The more vivid and detailed the visualization, the better. Envisaging the final product or outcome in all its glory is a sure-fire way of motivating you into action.

Although it takes time and patience, visualization is a powerful skill to master. "Seeing" peace, harmony, happiness, and success in your mind's eye will help you stay focused on your goal.

Bring attractive pictures and items into your living and workspaces. These will help to set the scene for positive thoughts.

Set aside at least 15 minutes daily to concentrate on positive thoughts and actions that will bring you success and happiness (Pietrzak, 2019).

Some of the things you may want to visualize might include:

- A new, happy and fulfilling relationship

- Improved working conditions

- The opportunity to start your own business

- A relaxing vacation

- The opportunity to live abroad

- A new, improved home

- Earning sufficient money to be able to live without financial worries

With consistent positive thoughts about the wonderful ideas you visualize becoming yours, fill your mind and heart with peace, harmony, and a sense of sincere gratitude. Genuine heartfelt desires will eventually become reality.

Follow these steps to help you get the most out of your visualizations:

Positive and Present

Keep your visualizations positive and word them in the present. For example, "I am not a failure," "I am capable of being an entrepreneur," or "I am attractive and worthy of a happy relationship."

Supportive Sensation

Support every visualization with a positive feeling. Make a conscious effort to replace your previously negative emotions into positive ones. The more support you bring your visualization, the better.

Repetition Is the Key

Consistent repetition is key to success. Remind yourself every day "I know that what I believe and say will become real."

Understanding that visualization is no "quick-fix" solution will help you realize that you need to put in consistent and constant effort if you want to see and experience positive change in your life.

Brain Training

Your subconscious mind can be trained and educated to change its thought patterns through the use of audio stimuli that alters brain waves. This may sound as though you are messing with nature, but the positive outcomes outweigh any concerns.

Your brain emits a number of different, measurable waves. These include:

- Alpha waves - these are emitted during periods of relaxation and quiet contemplation such as meditation.

- Beta waves - these are the waves emitted when you are active and fully engrossed in tasks such as reading or studying.

- Delta waves - these are emitted during periods when you are deeply asleep.

- Gamma waves - these are evident when you are busy with motor tasks, such as riding your bicycle, jogging, and working out at the gym.

- Theta waves - these waves are emitted when you are feeling drowsy or just falling to sleep.

The brain training program makes use of binaural beats, which involves playing two tones at differing frequencies. These have the power to alter or reprogram your normal brain waves to suit your needs. So, for example, if you wanted to relax, you would choose to listen to sounds that will encourage ALPHA waves and thus induce a state of relaxation.

The value of wave reprogramming

This positive method of intervention in reprogramming your brain waves helps to create a more receptive environment in your subconscious mind for the development of positive messages. The subconscious mind is more receptive to change during the alpha and theta states.

Hypnosis

During hypnosis, your subconscious mind is subjected to auto-suggestion during a period of relaxation. Continuous positive messages are streamed into your brain through your auditory channel.

Hypnosis can be done by a trained hypnotist or via pre-recorded audio programs that you can use in the comfort of your own home.

Unlocking the Power of Your Mind

By mastering the technique of releasing the power of your subconscious mind, you enable yourself to tap into the endless resources and potential hidden therein.

Tuning in to the power of your mind

Successfully unlocking your mind power requires that you are able to tune in to or access your subconscious mind. This is accomplished by deep breathing and transitioning into a state of peaceful relaxation. From this state, you can pursue almost any suitable goal you desire, from self-healing to attracting a special someone into your life, and from developing entrepreneurial skills to becoming a multimillionaire. The choice is yours!

Self-healing

You become more intuitive about your own health and make a better choice of lifestyle by ridding yourself of old, unhealthy habits and embracing exercise, good eating routines, and improving your overall general health.

Developing a greater sense of empathy toward others

Exercising the power of the mind enables you to embark on a more empathetic journey with other people based on a deeper understanding of the human condition and its frailties.

Improving your memory and clarity of thought

By tapping into the resources in your subconscious, you strengthen your memory skills and have the ability to think more clearly. You are no longer bogged down by the resistance of your mind.

Enhancing your creative abilities

Freedom from the fetters of your memories and fear allows you the chance to expand your creative horizon.

Developing improved concentration and focus

Your subconscious mind is the power-house of your very being, giving you the chance to focus on your goals and plan sensible routes to reach these.

Learning to identify and understand the root of your fears

Being in tune with yourself enables you to live a calmer life, free from many of the anxieties and fears that may previously have haunted you. When you are in a positive, relaxed state, it is easier to identify the cause of your fears and to think of possible ways to overcome these fears. Somehow, fear tends to reduce as soon as we recognize it for what it really is.

Monitoring the Success of the Reprogramming Process

Being able to monitor the progress of your subconscious retraining program is somewhat of a challenge. However, when you realize you are beginning to experience a positive change of heart toward yourself, you may also begin to:

- Think more positively about yourself

- Experience greater happiness and feel more confident

- Find yourself more enthusiastic to take up a challenge

- Begin to believe in yourself

- Feel calmer and more in control of your life

- Realize that you are no longer feeling overcome and anxious about changes

- Attract more good things in your life

Change does not happen immediately

Because change doesn't happen overnight, you may be disappointed. However, small changes will begin to occur and very often these may be witnessed by other people. The more you keep practicing, the better and the more noticeable the results will become.

Patience and practice and your full commitment to the program are at the core of your success.

The Important Takeaway Message

You now have a better understanding of the important role your subconscious mind plays in your life and that you have the power to reprogram your neural pathways to create a more positive platform from which to develop your successful goals.

Chapter 5:

The Positive Effects of Subconscious Reprogramming on Your Life

The mind is everything. What you think, you become."
– Gautama Buddha

Reprogramming your subconscious mind is not an easy task as the mind has many built-in security measures to stop unwanted access to the private information housed within its depths. However, it can certainly give you the edge over your competitors when it comes to applying for a job or starting your own enterprise. You only have to look at the example set by people like Steve Jobs, Richard Branson, and Oprah Winfrey to realize the power of focus and self-trust.

So, let us take a look at the control you can gain over your life with specific reference to your career.

Subconscious Reprogramming and Your Career

How do you think successful people land good jobs and have the capacity to earn the type of income you have only dreamt of?

Some of these individuals may have been fortunate enough to have been born into money, but for many others, they have become successful on their own.

One of our greatest stumbling blocks to success is our own attitude. We often "shoot ourselves in the foot," so to speak, before we have even left the first base.

Why are we guilty of self-sabotage?

For the majority of us, overcoming self-doubt is a huge challenge. We may have lived with the constant nagging of others in our family, school, or workplace who have undermined our faith and trust in our own abilities. The weight of all these negative words has filtered into your subconscious mind and become a proverbial "ball and chain."

Deep down in your heart, you know you have skills and the power to bring these to fruition if only you are given a break.

Well, let me remind you that you are in charge of your life. Because you know yourself better than anyone else on the earth does, you have the power to change your circumstances by altering your outlook and developing a more positive attitude to yourself and your opportunities for success.

The power of your mind can work in one of two ways. It can break you down and lead you into depression and thus destroy your chances of success. Or, it can build you up, uplift your spirit, fill you with enthusiasm, and the drive to follow your dream. It is up to you how you want to see your life play out.

Remember that very little success comes to those who sit around with expectant attitudes but no drive or enthusiasm. To be successful, you have to step out of your comfort zone and become a go-getter rather than an accepter.

Here are some stories of everyday people, like you and I, who have learned the art of reprogramming their subconscious mind for the good.

My friend Janet has focused on winning the final cycling event of the year in her cycling club. Before every event, she finds a quiet place to focus and imagine herself being victorious and carrying home the gold cup. She has always finished in the top three at every cycle meeting. She firmly believes that added to her hours of cycling practice as well as her attention to diet and exercise in the gym, her ability to focus on winning is what keeps her on top form. It was, therefore, no surprise to me when I watched her finish the final race to take first place.

At medical school, a student named Richard seemed to be coping very well despite his mother's nagging at him to study harder and stay focused. One day, just before his final exam, I found him sitting with his books and staring into space. When I inquired whether he was okay, his response was, "Oh, yes. I'm visualizing possible questions and the answers I believe will be best." I must admit I was taken aback by his laid back attitude. He passed his finals cum laude and is now a well-respected physician.

In both instances, added to their efforts, these people used the power of visualization to reach their goals. By reprogramming their subconscious into a positive mindset, they realized their goals and emerged victoriously.

Ideas on How to Achieve These Positive Results

- **Visualize yourself reaching your goal**

Visualization is perhaps the most powerful mental tool for realizing your dreams. If you can see it, you can believe it. This makes your goal real and tangible and, therefore, attainable.

Visualization directs your thoughts and planning in a specific direction which, in turn, leads your subconscious mind in the same direction.

Like Janet and Richard, visualize the positive result before the event and remain positive and focused on achieving the outcome you want.

By building a vivid, detailed mental picture of what you most want in life, you develop control over your subconscious mind making it believe in your goals and aligning itself with your desires.

Your subconscious can only work with finite, measurable data, so the clearer your mental pictures and the more precise your verbal explanation, the better. There is, then, no room for confusion. Your subconscious gets the pictures and will work to provide you with as much detail as necessary to achieve your goal.

The more you practice creative visualization, the more proficient you will become at picturing what you want to achieve in life, and in time, he who waits with patience and determination is successful.

- **Change your perception of yourself**

Closely linked to visualization is the need to review and then alter your perception of yourself, your circumstances, and your opportunities.

By learning to acknowledge your strengths and believing in yourself, your self-image begins to improve. Not only will you begin to feel better about who you are, but other people will begin to notice the change and become attracted to you.

Positive people attract other like-minded people into their circle of friends and associates.

You may have met people in your life who are always moaning about life and the "bad hand" they were dealt with. Generally, you begin to find excuses not to meet with these people, because their negativity depresses you.

• Stay on course

As with any plan of action, you are unlikely to be successful if you veer off-course.

Any Formula One racing driver will tell you that during a race you have to stay focused and concentrate on making tiny adjustments to the car as you drive around the track. Essentially, if you lose focus or fail to notice when to turn slightly left or right, or when to speed up or slow down, you are unlikely to successfully complete the race. Now, if you add your vision of winning a race of this nature, and you put every effort into realizing your dream, your chances improve exponentially.

• Keep up the positive talk

Continue to remind yourself that you have the skills and determination to see yourself reaching the position of CEO. Consistent affirmations of this positive nature will eventually train your subconscious into believing you are worthy of receiving what you ask for.

Fill your mind, thoughts, and dreams with a substantial increase in your paycheck. Reinforce these thoughts with words like, "I am going to be earning 50% more by the end of this year," or "Within three years, I will be the CEO of my own company."

Consistent positive thinking and speaking will train your subconscious to believe that what you are saying is true. According to Dr. Mona L. Schulz, "repetitive, positive affirmations" lead to "self-fulfilling prophecies" (Staff, n.d).

You will open yourself to new opportunities and be attractive to others seeking like-minded people for their businesses.

- **Keep a journal**

Keeping a written record of your dreams and positive comments about yourself may sound a bit far-fetched. However, when you re-read your notes, your subconscious absorbs the written words as confirmation of those that you have spoken.

Words, in both written and spoken form, are very powerful tools to help you reprogram your subconscious mind. They are the backbone of your communication with your fellow citizens as well as your family, friends, and colleagues.

The more precise, detailed, and organized your writing, the clearer the mental picture that will emerge. Remember, because your subconscious cannot distinguish reality from fiction, you can train it to believe anything you desire is possible.

- **Tune into your intuition**

By tuning into your intuition through meditation, you offer your subconscious the opportunity to become more receptive to positive thoughts, clear mental pictures, and a chance to upgrade all this important information that you will require for attaining your goals.

- **Hypnosis**

Moving on from the written word, hypnosis can be useful for training your mind to believe in your dreams.

You can either try visiting a professional hypnotist or make use of self-hypnosis techniques that come in the form of apps for cell phones or computers, or CDs or MP3s.

Hypnosis has a number of significant outcomes, among which are the following:

1. Relaxation of body and mind

2. Restoration of energy

3. Instilling peace

4. Improving focus and concentration

5. Aiding visualization

Always remember, you are smarter and more capable than you may think. You have the potential to achieve the dreams in your heart if you are prepared to make the effort to accept the challenge and give life your very best shot.

Preparation of a Resumé

When job searching, your resumé says a lot about you. If you are really serious about the job you have applied for, make sure your resumé fits who you really are.

Remember, your prospective employer has no idea of who you are and what you are capable of doing. It is essential therefore to ensure as much information is supplied in the resumé. However, your wording is of vital importance too. Try to avoid generalizations. Be more specific and let people know what your achievements are.

Customizing your resumé is vital for the application you are submitting. Most of the applications received may initially be assessed by a computerized robotic mechanism that scans the document for keywords. Ensure you understand the scope of the job and include as many suitable keywords as possible, which you may find in the advertisement.

In the event of your resumé making it to the next level of human contact, you should ensure you have written a well-structured, grammatically correct letter. You will have laid out your details as well as your qualifications with the prospective job in mind.

This is where you need to talk positive words and think uplifting thoughts about yourself so that your subconscious becomes filled with unequivocal ideas about you.

Then, you will be well prepared for the interview that lies ahead.

Subconscious Reprogramming for Wealth and Success

For many people, improving their financial status is a long-held desire, but their efforts have been fruitless. The challenge in most of these cases is the blockades that their subconscious mind has erected. Consciously, you may want to grow your wealth and become successful, but your subconscious mindset creates traps and so you don't make the progress you should.

It is important to realize the power of your subconscious mind needs to be released in order for you to be able to utilize this amazing force for your own benefit.

Margaret M. Lynch, a well-known author who believes that Emotional Freedom Techniques (EFT) make use of inner transformation to create visible, tangible wealth and success. Her insights on how to change your wealth programming process include five important strategies (Lynch & Schwartz, 2014).

According to Margaret, money has a mind and substance of its own. In other words, it is more than a thought or an idea.

During our lifetime. we have been subjected to see money as a commodity to be earned and used to purchase what we need and want. However, Margaret suggests we should view money in a different way.

She has five valuable disciplines to share, that if practiced daily, can bring better results than you may have ever imagined possible.

1. Your current financial status is one of your own making

Take a good, thorough look at your current financial status. Include all your earnings and how much you have managed to save, as well as all your debt. Make a clear note of all your assets and liabilities. Now, most of us understand these figures in terms of external criteria, such as our salary, lifestyle, inflation and interest rates, which are all external factors. However, when you view your money differently by realizing you started out with preconceived ideas of how your money should be handled, you suddenly realize you are in control and have been all along, without being aware.

This is a real wake-up call because you now realize that what you do with what you earn will be what brings you ultimate financial success or failure (Lynch & Schwartz, 2014).

2. Create a clear view of your money situation

As with all things learned, the pattern of handling money issues has been passed down from your family.

In many instances, family squabbles are often over money or the lack of it. Think back to your parents' views on this commodity. Try to recall how they dealt with paying bills and savings. Were there more bills to meet than income could provide for? And what were the bills? Standard rent or mortgage, no doubt, as well as food and utilities. What about schooling, clothing, and gas?

Once you have a picture of the approach your parents had to money, you will have a better understanding of how you see money and whether you value it as a commodity to be spent as soon as it is received, or maybe saved religiously for the proverbial "rainy day" (Lynch & Schwartz, 2014).

Our childhood view of money is all we have to use for our own financial planning. With no disrespect to our parents, who developed their view of money from their own family before that, we need to stop and realize that if we want to become wealthier than we are now, our view of money and how we handle it has to change.

3. Pinpoint your personal financial issues

We have all, for the most part, suffered financial trauma to a greater or lesser degree. Pinpoint those areas and decide if they still have the power to hold you back. Are you maybe still harboring doubts, fears, anger, or even a sense of failure because of these instances when your finances went "pear-shaped"?

The minute you realize these issues have passed, the only thing you can do is to acknowledge their presence. However, the plan is now to move on with a more positive approach by deciding on instituting an active strategy to decrease the debt and increase your savings.

4. Use powerful mind-body techniques to develop a positive mindset

Most people are like trapped antelope, cornered by a predator. Our adrenaline begins to spike the minute we have to work with money matters. We are fearful and filled with angst. What if the antelope suddenly and unexpectedly charged the predator? An unlikely scenario, I know, but what if? The predator may possibly be shocked into backing off, perhaps giving the antelope a chance to escape.

So too, when you confront your money issues head-on, you may find they are not as frightening as you first imagined. And, with careful and consistent planning, you can bring them under control in less time than you would have done if you had let the problem continue to snowball.

A great way to bring your mind and body into line is to practice "tapping," according to Margaret. Tapping on your acupuncture points helps to calm your body and mind giving you the opportunity to discover, like the antelope, that window of opportunity for escape. Escape in the sense of finding a solution to your financial woes rather than running away and ignoring them (Lynch & Schwartz, 2014).

5. Set new money goals

Using obsolete systems stunt your chance for keeping up with modern technology and being able to compete in the twenty-first century with business opportunities and growing your wealth and assets.

So too, outdated views on your handling money do nothing more than add to your stress and potential poverty.

Using your conscious power, judge the status of your finances. Realize your worth and know that you should be earning more for your efforts if, of course, you really do put in the effort. Then, look for ways to improve your income. Can you ask for a raise or should you consider a second job? Whatever your decision, ensure you make an effort to settle your debt as soon as possible and start saving more than you would normally have done.

Consider investing in some "smart money" strategies to help you achieve your wealth-goals. If you find you are unable to make head-way, seek professional help to clear your mind of the residual emotions creating obstacles to your success (Lynch & Schwartz, 2014).

Develop New Neural Pathways for Success

Your brain develops new neural pathways as it learns new information every day through your interaction with your environment via your senses, emotions, speech, and thoughts, as well as your behavior. This process involving the development of new pathways is known in scientific terms as neuroplasticity.

Your knowledge can be utilized to either enhance reality or distort it, according to your needs. When you enable your subconscious to rule, the information is often not as true a reflection of your reality as you might like to believe.

Why is this the case?

Your subconscious mind is full of prejudice and preconceived ideas, out of which, it fabricates its own reality.

When you take control of your subconscious, you disallow your mind to divert your attention because you are its master, and it becomes subservient to your commands.

Okay, so if you control your mind, you can, in essence, program it to think and plan as you wish?

To a large degree, this idea is correct; however, not everyone has the power to command their own subconscious. Those that develop this control often have the power to control other people around them as well.

This is exactly the plan behind those seductive advertisements you often see, each trying its level best to persuade or cajole you into believing you desperately need the product, goods, or technology that is advertised.

This type of mental messaging that has the power to undermine your better judgment is called subliminal control and can be seriously detrimental to us, the buying public.

However, when you are behind the controls of your own subconscious, this is a powerful position to hold. You can decide how best to meet your personal needs and desires by coercing your subconscious to play the correct role to get you to your destination without too much hardship (Lynch & Schwartz, 2014).

Where to begin?

So, in the words of Richard Bach, "To bring anything into your life, imagine that it's already there" (Kaur, et al., 2018).

Now, the important thing to remember here is to differentiate between positive optimism and downright arrogance. If you know you have studied hard in preparation for, let's say your Science exam, you may feel optimistic about the outcome. However, if you haven't opened a book but arrogantly believe you will pass anyway, although the outcomes may be the same, the methodology in the second instance may have been subject to your great skills at visualizing a pass mark.

For the majority of people, the second option is most unlikely to end so successfully; however, with effort and positive mind control, you can visualize anything into your control.

Sound a bit fuzzy to you? Give it a try and really put your back into it before you decide if visualization and subconscious reprogramming are worthwhile strategies for you.

Margaret Lynch, a well-respected self-help coach, uses the power of inner transformation to create external wealth and success. She has made use of the same techniques and has established a million-dollar business assisting and advising clients to achieve wealth and success (Lynch & Schwartz, 2014).

Recognize and identify the thoughts and words that bring you down

Saying hurtful things to yourself only affects you and breaks down your self-esteem and confidence.

Each one of us gets irritated by some of the silly things we find ourselves doing. Instead of berating yourself, try to look at the situation objectively and decide the "why."

Negative thoughts are a challenge to deal with because they tend to latch into your subconscious.

As soon as you become aware of negative thoughts, feelings, or words, STOP and breathe before you continue. When you identify the source of these sensations, you are better able to avoid them in the future and thus protect yourself from falling into their trap.

The first step is to train your subconscious not to pay attention to the negatives by feeding it as much positive information and increasing the good sensations at the same time. With continued efforts of this kind, your subconscious will soon differentiate between what it enjoys and finds exciting and the negatives that it now views as useless information.

Tackle problems early

As soon as you become aware of a problem or challenge, face it head-on and try to find a resolution as soon as possible. The longer problems lie unsolved, the larger they appear to grow until they reach proportions beyond your capabilities to resolve.

Many of our problems appear huge and daunting to start with, but as soon as we make an effort to resolve them, they often begin to diminish.

The best way to tackle a problem is to use your analytical and creative skills. Assess the problem and identify its source. Then, use your imagination to solve it. These skills differentiate successful people from the crowd.

Keep asking yourself how the solution to the problematic situation can benefit you. Most successful entrepreneurs have faced their problems with an open mind and used all their energy and brainstorming skills to reach a solution (Lynch & Schwartz, 2014).

Make a note of the problems you faced and the solutions you found for each. Keep a record of these "mental transactions" in your journal as a documented reminder of how far you have come.

According to George Lois, "Creativity can solve almost any problem" (Kaur, et al., 2018).

Practice meditation and get physical

Regular exercise in any form is a great booster for blood circulation, and in turn, for oxygenating the brain. The positive impact of exercise on our brain leads to improved blood supply and greater clarity of thought.

Exercise requires concentration and commitment. It is an excellent way to train your brain and encourage your subconscious to get off its proverbial "couch" and into its groove.

Meditation has been practiced for centuries and is a guaranteed way for you to find inner peace and harmony with the Universe.

Meditation also helps to train your mind to focus, without interruption on a specific topic or idea. This action brings you closer to achieving your dreams and goals.

Train your mind with brain exercises

Crossword puzzles, reading, problem-solving puzzles, and mental mathematical calculations are a good start to get the neuro-jelly wobbling at full speed.

Brain exercises strengthen your IQ and capacity to think logically. Active minds that are intellectually inquisitive are less likely to fall victim to aging diseases.

Subconscious Reprogramming for Relationships

Relationships are perhaps one of the most complicated matters humans have to deal with. Different personalities and backgrounds make each of us unique individuals in our own right.

Are you stuck in a relationship that's going nowhere?

Maybe you are stuck in a relationship that has failed, or you would like to approach a certain someone whom you find attractive, but you are afraid of rejection. Whatever your situation, your subconscious mind is more than likely the culprit for your distress.

Okay, so how does this all work? Well, according to Bruce H. Lipton, during the "honeymoon phase" of your relationship, your conscious mind is in control, directing your emotions and attitude out of the need for companionship and love. However, after a time, the conscious mind tires of having to keep the romantic ship afloat, and it relinquishes its control to your subconscious mind because it has more pressing day-to-day matters to deal with (Lipton, .n.d).

Pre-Programmed Behavior Sets In

Now your subconscious mind is pre-programmed with all your memories and past experiences in the field of relationships, both successful and failed. This area of your mind perceives the obstacles to the relationship and throws up all sorts of challenges, many based on prior misconceptions. Now, your relationship that you believed was made in heaven begins to flounder, and you can't quite figure out why.

Suddenly, there are four minds active in this romantic liaison. Two of these are the subconscious entity of each partner in the relationship. As soon as the conscious mind recedes, it takes the glow and positive sheen off the relationship, leaving the subconscious in control.

Now, all you have witnessed in prior relationships between parents, family members, friends, and colleagues are being used subconsciously as your frame of reference.

You begin to notice flaws in your partner and perhaps some of your own shortcomings too, of which you were previously unaware. Collectively, these negative vibes begin to degrade and corrode your relationship until it lies in total tatters, leaving you perhaps shell-shocked and completely unprepared for the nasty outcome either in the divorce court or being left with nothing but the clothes you are wearing. From 100 to zero in a very short time.

Vital ways to reprogram your mind for success

It is important to change your mindset if you are seeking success in any form, be it from increasing wealth to improving your relationships.

Be mindful of what you ask for

If you don't have a clear mental picture of the type of person you would like to meet and get to know, you can't expect the Universe, or anyone else for that matter, to know either.

Be as clear and concise with your idea of the ideal person for you. By picturing that person, your conscious mind stores the image in the subconscious for future ratification, and you will, in all likelihood, get what you asked for.

Appraise your subconscious programming technique

Check to see what sort of behavior you display and decide whether it is the best for attracting the type of person you hope to meet.

We are all governed by our history of relationships and the "relationship formula" set by our parents. By making a concerted effort to assess yourself and then decide on the type of ideal partner you would like to have, you allow yourself to reprogram some of the preconceived ideas stored in your subconscious.

The greatest challenge with this sort of appraisal is that your honesty is of paramount importance. Each of us has flaws we know about and possibly many more that we are unaware of.

By being willing to mend our own flaws we allow ourselves to repair past damage and start afresh.

Rid yourself of old hurts

Old hurts and memories from your history are raised into your consciousness when you consider a relationship. These memories create anxiety and a sense of insecurity that hold you back from pursuing your goal.

If you are able to dip into the techniques of the Law of Attraction, you will certainly learn to bend your mind's will to suit your own needs. This may sound a bit far-fetched, but we all have the innate power to make certain things happen in our lives.

The Important Takeaway Message

Subconscious reprogramming to embrace new opportunities

The subconscious mind, although well-stocked with every scrap of your personal information, does not have the ability to distinguish between fiction and reality. With this in mind, you have the power to exercise your own reality over your subconscious. You need to be sharp about this plan, though, because the subconscious mind has a veritable army of resources at its disposal that draws on all the time for added support and manipulation of your ideas and thoughts.

So, if you have been told that something is unlikely to occur, say a pregnancy, for example, you want to give up trying, right? Yup, for many people that is exactly what they will do. Here is the story of someone who would not give up.

My dear friend Frances, married for almost 10 years and up to that point childless, longed for a baby. She underwent every conceivable test only to find she was in good health and therefore quite capable of bearing a child.

One day, Frances met a woman who told her to remain positive and to visualize herself holding a baby of her own. Frances decided this plan was worth a try as she had nothing to lose. For the next three years, Frances held the vision in her heart and mind of a tiny, perfect baby girl. Eventually, Frances received the great news that she was expecting and delivered that perfect, tiny girl.

The power of positive thinking and visualization can change your life for the better.

Chapter 6:

Healing from Trauma through Subconscious Reprogramming

Understanding How Trauma Impacts Us

Trauma refers to an often unexpected and profoundly hurtful or damaging experience that leaves the sufferer shocked and deeply distressed. Generally, trauma not only affects us physically, as in broken bones or a severe head injury, but it can cause serious psychological harm.

Trauma is a normal reaction

It should be clarified that trauma is a natural reaction to an unnatural, unexpected, horrifying event.

A traumatic event can be in the form of a one-time horrific incident, such as the sudden and unexpected death of a child. Or trauma can be the result of ongoing, multiple events, such as those experienced by women and children who are assaulted in their homes by another family member. Trauma can also come from multiple agonizing and frightening incidents, such as those experienced by men at war.

Every individual will at some point in their lifetime experience some sort of traumatic event. This could take the form of a car accident or a medical emergency. It could be as a result of a fire or a natural disaster. In some instances, trauma comes as a result of combat injuries, assault, abuse, or even a robbery.

Being a witness to a traumatic event also leaves the onlooker in a state of shock.

The symptoms of psychological trauma

- Generally, people who suffer trauma are in a state of shock and disbelief.

- They may experience confusion, and in some instances, they may have difficulty concentrating on what needs to be done.

- Sometimes, trauma results in severe outbursts of uncontrolled anger. People may also display irritability or unusual mood swings.

- In most cases, there will be feelings of anxiety and deep fear as well as a sense of being "under fire."

- Depending on the traumatic incident, people may experience feelings of guilt, shame, and even self-blame.

- Victims of trauma often become withdrawn and show no desire to communicate with other people, because there is a sense of disconnection from society.

- They may feel terribly sad, lonely, and may even contemplate suicide.

How we react to trauma

There are few people who can admit to never having experienced any form of trauma in their lifetime. Trauma in one form or another is the unfortunate by-product of the world in which we live.

Some of the people who suffer trauma remain capable of outwardly hiding their symptoms of distress and can, in some instances, live their entire lives without admitting their pain. It must, however, be added here that these people are most likely not living their best life.

Other people who are the victims of traumatic events, may exhibit symptoms of Post Traumatic Stress Disorder (PTSD) and may also seek support to help them deal with their stress and pain.

Survival response to trauma

Survivors react after any traumatic is complicated and intensely personal. This is due to each person's own experiences, their subconscious responses in the face of disaster to be able to cope under frightening circumstances, and their support system.

Each individual will display their own response to the event as well as their personal coping mechanism. And, each response is perfectly normal for the individual and should be viewed as such.

The most important factor here is to ensure the coping mechanism is in line with safety and that it will in way jeopardize any further trauma.

So, for example, if a child drowns in the ocean, the parents will more than likely display huge shock, disbelief, and grief.

Some survivors are capable of dealing with their trauma alone, without professional advice, while others require either short or long-term clinical help and debriefing support.

Although most people don't dwell on thoughts of death, the result of any traumatic episode for those who survive is to experience a sudden and revealing realization that life is limited and that we are mortal. Sometimes, this knowledge spurs individuals into action to make something of their lives. These people allow the emotional trauma to work for their success by turning the negative scenario into something positive.

Symptoms that survivors may experience

The usual initial response to trauma may include a sense of confusion or dissociation and great sadness. Survivors may also experience anxiety, slight to extreme agitation, and exhaustion.

For the majority of people, these symptoms are quite normal and considered socially acceptable because they alleviate immediate stress and help the survivor cope. They are also generally self-limited in that the survivor resorts to this behavior for relatively short periods.

However, when the survivor is unable to respond to any exterior advice or support due to extended periods of distress without intervening rest, or they display severe dissociation and continued periods of recall of the trauma, expert support is required.

In some instances, survivors may suffer a delayed response to the traumatic event. These are usually evident in the continued feelings of fatigue, interrupted sleep patterns, as well as nervous twitches and anxiety attacks.

Diagnosing Trauma Sufferers

The challenge in diagnosing people suffering from the stress that results from trauma lies in the fact that the impact of trauma can be either cunningly devious, or flagrantly devastating. This all depends on the person's reaction to the event, the characteristics of the circumstances, the significance of the trauma, as well as the physical environment in which the trauma occurred.

Whatever the source of the trauma, an indelible imprint is left on our brain, which we will require professional help to deal with. When you experience any kind of trauma, there is immediately increased activity in the areas in your brain that process shock, fear, and anxiety.

Post-traumatic stress disorder and acute stress disorder

Because humans are a lot more resilient than we may at first imagine, most survivors who exhibit immediate symptoms to the traumatic event, generally resolve their emotional response over a period of time. Although the memory does not necessarily disappear, it will usually fade and become a manageable memory. Their stress levels decrease, and they may be able to talk about the incident without reliving the terror.

There are, however, those survivors who appear to be coping well for short periods of time but who then "crack up" for no apparent reason are more than likely suffering from trauma and stress-related disorders, such as acute stress disorder (ASD) or post-traumatic stress disorder. Many war veterans may fall into this category.

Specific Reactions to a Traumatic Event

The number of responses to trauma varies depending on the individuals involved. However, this is not to say these sufferers exhibit signs of mental illness or disorders. Some simply require more thorough support and professional guidance than others to overcome their stresses and fears (Center for Substance Abuse Treatment, US, 1970).

Some of the common responses include:

Emotional Responses

These reactions vary according to an individual's sociocultural background. Therefore, people who have learned that it is unacceptable or considered too dangerous to display their emotions in public will attempt to maintain a "stiff upper lip" for fear of embarrassment or negative repercussions.

Other survivors may refuse to discuss their feelings, denying they have any or may readily admit to being too numb to be able to respond further.

Emotional disorganization

In some instances, survivors may display emotional disorganization, in which they have difficulty controlling their anger, anxiety, and fear, or perhaps feelings of shame. These people may develop substance abuse habits, self-mutilation, or eating disorders to help them cope. The challenge in these instances is that the intended self-help remedy usually back-fires and adds untold misery and further complications to their lives.

There are, however, survivors who willingly and consciously take on tasks requiring mental, and in some cases, physical effort to overcome their stress, anxiety, and fear. These people use negative events as a springboard to create something positive and lasting (Center for Substance Abuse Treatment, US, 1970).

Fear and anxiety

Fear and anxiety are often on-going side-shows after a trauma that can create untold stress for survivors. Sometimes, the fear abates after a period, while at other times, it rears its head at the most inconvenient opportunities (Gillihan, 2016).

Anger

Anger is perhaps one of the most common natural human responses to trauma. We may experience this emotion toward ourselves if we believe we were in some way responsible for the traumatic event (Gillihan, 2016).

For example, we may have witnessed a vehicle accident and feel we could somehow have warned the pedestrian who was severely injured.

Or, as ridiculous as it may sound, we may feel anger toward the event itself, as in a hurricane, for destroying our property.

Sadness

Feelings of sadness and heartache are part and parcel of any trauma. These emotions are sometimes difficult to control as they pop up at inopportune moments and may cause us embarrassment.

Tears are the response of the parasympathetic nervous system, which acts to calm the body down after stress (Gillihan, 2016).

Overwhelming sadness and grief are also ways in which the mind attempts to reach an understanding of the event to deal with it appropriately.

Guilt and blame

Many survivors struggle with feelings of guilt, and some carry the blame for the incident. This is often the case in which a family member, in particular a child, has been injured or killed. Parents and siblings may wonder what they could have done differently to avoid the loss of their loved one.

Guilt and blame often lead to self-recrimination, which may eventually corrode your self-confidence.

Lack of trust

There is a definite lack of trust that develops in a trauma survivor. As in the case of Lisa, a bartender, who was brutally beaten and raped by a group of drunken men. Lisa now finds it a challenge to be in the company of the opposite sex and seldom leaves her tiny apartment, because even walking past a man on the sidewalk brings all her anguish and pain flooding back.

Unrealistic fear

Sometimes, the aftermath of trauma leaves the survivor with residual anxiety that can be triggered by a noise or sudden movement. For example, a door slamming can trigger a memory of a gunshot.

Physical Responses

Some survivors display physical symptoms long after the event. These may take the form of sweating, sleep disorders, bedwetting, skin allergies, or gastrointestinal disturbances, among others.

Where these symptoms continue unabated despite treatment, the underlying emotional trauma is usually the reason.

Nightmares and disturbed sleep

Recurring nightmares may haunt a survivor's sleep. These are often on-going and can become more creative and frightening if they are not curtailed as quickly as possible.

Numbness

After a traumatic event, survivors may experience a feeling of numbness and a disjointed sense of reality.

Living on your toes

Stress can sometimes leave the person with a feeling of insecurity that makes them constantly look over their shoulder so that they can be ready for flight if more trauma comes their way.

Cognitive Responses

Many individuals who are survivors of some trauma have an altered outlook on life. Where they may have been carefree, cheerful people before the event, they now live in constant fear. The smallest changes in their perception of their environment can turn any previously acceptable situation into a living nightmare for them.

Difficulty interpreting data

Generally, people who suffer from cognitive issues due to past trauma have difficulty clearly interpreting current situations. They may have irrational fears or excessive feelings of guilt.

Recurring memories

They may also suffer hallucinations and be unable to forget the event that occurred because they continue to replay the memories.

Flash-backs

These people often suffer "flash-backs" that are triggered by almost insignificant stimuli to non-sufferers (Center for Substance Abuse Treatment, US, 1970).

Behavioral Responses

Continued reminiscing and re-enactment of the scenario fit people in this category as they try to come to terms with what happened and somehow take ownership of the event.

Self-mutilation

All too often, these survivors end up either self-mutilating, substance abuse, behaving in dangerous ways, or continually being involved in on-going abusive relationships.

Dangerous behavior

Trauma survivors may sometimes become involved in dangerous behavior, such as reckless car racing, skydiving, or stunt acting. Their need to test their morality may drive them to make foolish decisions that may not end well.

Recurring abusive relationships

Women survivors of abuse are often drawn into a new abusive relationship. These people seem to believe they are not worthy of anything better. They may also feel that they failed before and that perhaps if they have another chance, they may have the power to change their partner's behavior.

Avoidance

In certain serious cases, survivors may decide to live life as a recluse, avoiding all contact with other people. They may even decide to drop-out of traditional society to live on the streets.

Adaptable Responses to Traumatic Events

A great many survivors discover meaningful, positive ways in which to cope with trauma and thereby heal themselves and restore their equilibrium.

In many cases, people inevitably re-evaluate their lives, including their values and what defines them as individuals.

Their resilience affords them the opportunity to start afresh and to move in a positive direction, feeling uplifted and positive about their future.

These are the people who instinctively know they need to retrain their subconscious to recreate a brighter outlook on life (Center for Substance Abuse Treatment, US, 1970).

Improved bonding

Many survivors rejoice that they are alive and re-evaluate their personal relationships with family and friends. They may take better care of their children and value their partner more.

The loss of a loved one can bring a family closer together.

Developing a sense of purpose

Trauma has a way of raising the mortality flag for us all. The sudden realization that we are transient beings in this world may prompt some people to seek out a specific task in which they feel they are giving something back to society or just simply making a difference (Center for Substance Abuse Treatment, US, 1970).

Increased commitment

Survivors may opt for making more of a commitment to their fellow workers or family members by sacrificing something they previously held dear. Their loyalty and sense of responsibility may improve as they make an effort to support others in need (Center for Substance Abuse Treatment, US, 1970).

Amended priorities

People who, previous to the trauma, may have put their wealth or status first may now realize that life, family, and friendship is more important.

Improved charity

For the most part, many survivors stretch their hand out to others in need. They are caring and show empathy to those suffering in a similar way to themselves.

They may volunteer their time as a lifeguard after a drowning, or become a support firefighter after a devastating fire. They may choose to help in a shelter or grow food to support the hungry. There are so many ways in which people can volunteer their services and support for those in need (Center for Substance Abuse Treatment, US, 1970).

Trauma and Brain Function

Severe trauma can adversely affect the brain in a number of ways. There are, however, three main important areas to consider:

The prefrontal cortex (PFT)

This area, located behind your forehead near the top of your head is where our thinking, planning, and problem-solving takes place. It is also associated with our personality, feelings of empathy, and attitude toward others.

The anterior cingulate cortex (ACC)

This is the center that regulates our emotions, generally keeping them in check, and which is situated deep in our brain next to the prefrontal cortex.

The amygdala

This very small, subcortical area, situated deep inside the brain is responsible for managing our fear.

The amygdala falls under the command of our subconscious, so we, therefore, have no direct control over its functioning.

All our sensory input passes through the amygdala, and it is here that decisions are made about the safety of what we see, hear, smell, taste, and feel. In the event of the amygdala detecting anything untoward about the stimuli it receives, it signals immediate danger to which we respond accordingly.

So, What's Actually Happening In a Traumatized Brain?

Traumatized people look and act differently than those who are not affected by trauma in one of three specific ways:

1. The prefrontal cortex is under activated.

2. The anterior cingulate cortex is under activated.

3. The amygdala is overactivated.

This simply means that the areas employed in higher-level activities are impaired while the "Fear Center" is highly activated.

This means that the person will be suffering symptoms of stress, probably a high level of fear, with possible side effects of unusual irritation bordering on anger.

This same individual will have difficulty concentrating and remaining focused on any task. They may complain of being unable to think clearly. This is a normal reaction when the *prefrontal cortex* (the thinking area) is under active because of the shock factor.

There will also be evidence of a possible breakdown in their emotional tolerance level, resulting in floods of tears and undue shock responses to hearing a loud noise or someone shouting. This is due to the weakened *anterior cingulate cortex* (center of emotions).

Reprogramming the Subconscious After Trauma

Many people choose to ignore their negative feelings, sometimes pushing these into the recesses of their minds in the hope that they will remain hidden.

Unfortunately, they will not. These emotions have a habit of bubbling to the surface when least expected where they recreate trauma of their own.

By far, the most sensible way to handle the aftermath of trauma and its ensuing emotional turmoil is to confront it head-on. So, before they get the chance to take control of your entire life, recognize the emotions you are experiencing and link them directly to the specific trauma in which you were involved.

Five Valuable Tips to Stimulate the Healing Power of Your Subconscious

1. Begin each new day with a "clean slate"

Clear your mind of negativity every morning before you start your day. Positive energy cannot occupy the same space as anger, hatred, and emotional turmoil. Now, think of happy, positive things that will draw good, creative energy into your space.

This is also a good time to consider any problems you are facing and think about possible solutions (Young, 2020).

2. Keep your thoughts positive and practice positive self-talk

Guard your thoughts and persevere in keeping them positive and constructive. Try not to allow negative thoughts or information to invade your space. The minute you experience a negative thought, physically stop yourself, breathe deeply, and fill your mind with something positive.

By refusing to entertain negative thoughts, you take control of your subconscious by persuading it to change its emotional status.

So, remain positive and hopeful, and your entire demeanor will begin to radiate these messages. The subconscious absorbs the good vibes and returns them, ten-fold.

3. Keep yourself fully occupied

Harness your subconscious mind's healing power by keeping yourself occupied during stressful times. The idiom, "The devil finds work for idle hands" generates great power over your mind when you don't have anything else to concentrate on besides your hardship.

So, think positive and act with confidence to give your mind the chance to heal.

4. Fill the space with relaxing, inspiring music

We live in busy, stressful times that often leave us little space for relaxation. Making time, particularly at the end of the day, to relax and unwind while you listen to soothing music, will afford you the opportunity to reduce the production of cortisol and restore the balance in your mental and physical state.

5. Yoga and meditation

For some people, yoga presents an excellent chance to restore their inner sense of balance. Yoga not only offers the opportunity for physical exercise but also mental and spiritual stress relief.

The Important Takeaway Message

Because your subconscious mind, which never takes a moment off from its duties, has guided and controlled you to date, according to its own plan of action, you have unknowingly fallen prey to its manipulative power.

Harnessing the power of your subconscious mind empowers you to take control of your life and destiny to overcome any obstacle with which you may be faced.

By being kind to yourself and practicing and implementing some of the suggested tips in this book *Human Mind Power: The Power of Your Subconscious Mind*, you will experience positive change in yourself, which will, in turn, alter your view of life for the better.

Conclusion

Each individual experiences fear in some form or another during their lives. This is because the subconscious is in control of our feelings and emotions. Our subconscious guides us in terms of what it judges good for our safety and well-being, even if its database is outdated.

Unless we decide to the contrary, our pre-programmed subconscious will continue its task of dominating us for the remainder of our lifetime. However, if we intend to make positive changes in our working environment, upgrade our personal relationships, improve our creative skills, and generally perk ourselves up, it is imperative that we take control of our subconscious.

We have covered a great deal of information on the function of the subconscious mind being the number one processor of all the information received via our conscious interaction with our environment.

It has been established that the subconscious mind is the seat of all your dreams, known and remembered, as well as those you will never recall. The subconscious never sleeps or rests but is constantly in motion, firing away to sort through and catalog information before storing it in its limitless vault.

Imagine being able to tap directly into this reservoir of amazing information and to use it to create wealth, stability, happiness, and success in your own life.

Ditch Your Pessimistic Outlook

A pessimistic mindset contradicts your efforts of reaching your goal. Negative thoughts need to be replaced by positive ideas, beliefs, and actions if you are to succeed.

To do this, you should refocus on your goals, ensure these are realistic and attainable, and then reprogram your brain to follow a new path toward success.

Undertaking retraining your subconscious mind is no walk in the park, but with consistent and dogged effort, you have a great chance of becoming the successful person you envisaged yourself to be.

Remember to be patient and to stay focused on the end goal. Stay determined and don't be swayed from your dreams.

Engage in plenty of positive affirmations. Acknowledge and take advantage of the power of your subconscious mind and put it to good use in leading you toward your goal.

Never Underestimate the Unlimited Power of Your Mind

We are not normally taught to access our subconscious potential, probably because so few people know how to achieve this in the first place. Mindpower is a strange, and for some people, an uncomfortable possibility.

Through harnessing the power of your mind, you allow your creativity free reign to build wonderful vistas and possibilities for success. Sometimes, these may seem quite impossible, but if you trust in the power you have stored in your subconscious and are willing to put in consistent effort to evoke these goals into reality, they are likely to come into being.

So, you want to lose weight. Focus on the mental picture of how you would like to look once you reach your goal. Keep that picture in your mind's eye as you begin the process of dieting and exercising until you reach your goal weight. Although this may sound simple, the process takes some time, but it works for those with the grit to stick to the program.

Having power over your mind increases your self-knowledge as well as your intuitive awareness of your strengths and willpower.

Mind Power Techniques

For the best results, always begin these techniques from a place of relaxation and peace. Start by finding a quiet area and get comfortable. Ensure the temperature is just right and that there is sufficient air circulation, but without a draught.

To avoid interference from your conscious mind, check that you have covered all bases for possible distractions, including the television, computer, iPad, and cell phone.

Express positive thoughts

Begin by expressing positive thoughts and words. Feed your heart and mind with these good vibes and envisage yourself in a happy, relaxed, and very positive space.

The law of attraction is a powerful technique that will come into play in a positive space. Be mindful of the things you would like to see happen in your life when you are relaxed. When you are positive, other people around you become more positive too. In this way, the positive energy increase exponentially.

Consciously monitor your thoughts and words. Build positive thoughts and repeat happy, healthy, self-fulfilling words and phrases. Discard all negative thoughts as they try to enter your conscious thoughts.

Express gratitude

Express gratitude for all you have right now, no matter how little that might actually be. Gratitude is a sign for the universe to bless you more abundantly.

The "creator mindset"

Develop a "creator mindset," says Andrew Shorten (Andrew Shorten Co-Founder of Greater Minds. Positive Thinker, 2019).

Each time you practice mind power, notice the creative ideas that come to the fore. Try to search through these ideas for one that particularly appeals to you and use it as the potential starting point for your next mindpower session.

Over a short period of time, you may find your creativity begins to grow and embellish this idea to form a viable and worthy goal to pursue.

For example, you may have an initial idea to start your own business. Your main interest is fashion, but you have not yet honed it down to a specific niche in the market. After a number of mindpower sessions, you experience a "light bulb" moment when your subconscious mind throws out a little gem of an idea in the form of "earrings." Gradually, the idea grows into a plan that you are able to execute.

You now have a lucrative business designing and creating beautiful ethnic earrings that are taking the fashion world by storm.

The entire process took a fair while to stabilize from the idea stage into something tangible and real, but now you are well on your way to opening another store in a second state. The power of the mind has once again delivered.

Behave as though you have achieved your goal

Positive behavior reinforces your hopes and dreams by showing yourself and those around you that you believe everything will fall into place as planned.

Envisage yourself at the height of your successful career or the recipient of that accolade you desire.

When you begin to think and act as though you have achieved your goal, the positive energy you exude works to draw the right people into your life. This, in turn, strengthens your belief in yourself and in your abilities. All-in-all, this is a positive place to be as you begin to achieve everything you dreamed of and more (Staff, n.d).

With all the information previously covered, you will by now realize that managing any kind of trauma takes time, effort, and a great deal of kindness and understanding.

Professional support

Psychotherapy and mindful-based training techniques, which include "diaphragmatic breathing and autogenic training" (Sweeton, 2017), may prove useful.

Chatting to someone you trust who is non-judgemental may also help.

Self-help apps

A number of useful self-help apps are available. Please visit the following website if you are interested. https://www.ptsd.va.gov/appvid/mobile/index.as p

References

Center for Substance Abuse Treatment (US). (1970, January 1). Understanding the Impact of Trauma. Retrieved March 10, 2020, from https://www.ncbi.nlm.nih.gov/books/NBK207191/

Cherry, K. (2019, June 15). The Structure and Levels of the Mind According to Freud. Retrieved from https://www.verywellmind.com/the-conscious-and-unconscious-mind-2795946

Gillihan, S. J. (2016, September 7). 21 Common Reactions to Trauma. Retrieved March 10, 2020, from https://www.psychologytoday.com/za/blog/think-act-be/201609/21-common-reactions-trauma

Henry Ford. (2020, February 27). Retrieved March 4, 2020, from https://en.wikipedia.org/wiki/Henry_Ford

Kaur, R., Thirupati, S., JAT, D., Veeranjaneyulu, V., Jha, A., Evan, … Eric. (2018, October 19). How To Hack Your Subconscious Mind for Massive Success. Retrieved March 7, 2020, from https://www.shoutmeloud.com/train-subconscious-mind-success.html

Kehoe, J. (n.d.). Mind Power Basics: Mind Power. Retrieved March 8, 2020, from https://www.learnmindpower.com/using-mind-power/basics/

Lipton, B. H. (n.d.). A Little Known Way To Improve Your Relationship. Retrieved March 8, 2020, from https://www.healyourlife.com/a-little-known-way-to-improve-your-relationship

Lynch, M. M., & Schwartz, D. D. (2014). Tapping into wealth: how Emotional Freedom Techniques (EFT) can help you clear the path to making more money. Retrieved March 13, 2020, from https://www.amazon.com/Tapping-Into-Wealth-Emotional-Techniques/dp/0399168826

ONeill, R. J. (2018, November 16). 3 Tips for Controlling the Subconscious Mind and Taking Control of Your Life. Retrieved March 9, 2020, from https://exemplore.com/new-age-metaphysics/3-Tips-for-Controlling-the-Subconscious-Mind

Pietrzak, M. (2019, February 7). 4 Ways to Actively Reprogram Your Thoughts. Retrieved March 9, 2020, from https://www.success.com/4-ways-to-actively-reprogram-your-thoughts/

Phillips, H. (2006, September 4). Introduction: The Human Brain. Retrieved March 2, 2020, from https://www.newscientist.com/article/dn9969-introduction-the-human-brain/

Richards, S. (n.d.). Mind Power Quotes (739 quotes). Retrieved March 8, 2020, from https://www.goodreads.com/quotes/tag/mind-power

Sohn, E. (2019, July 24). Decoding the neuroscience of consciousness. Retrieved March 1, 2020, from https://www.nature.com/articles/d41586-019-02207-1

Staff. (n.d.). How to Reprogram Your Subconscious Mind for Success and Happiness. Retrieved March 8, 2020, from https://greatperformersacademy.com/habits/how-to-reprogram-your-subconscious-mind-for-success-and-happiness

Subconscious. (2020, January 8). Retrieved February 29, 2020, from https://en.wikipedia.org/wiki/Subconscious

Sweeton, J. (2017, March 13). How to Heal the Traumatized Brain. Retrieved March 11, 2020, from https://www.psychologytoday.com/za/blog/workings-well-being/201703/how-heal-the-traumatized-brain

Tracy, B. (2018, December 12). The Power of Your Subconscious Mind: Brian Tracy. Retrieved March 1, 2020, from https://www.briantracy.com/blog/personal-success/understanding-your-subconscious-mind/

Wiest, B. (2018, September 12). 13 Ways To Start Training Your Subconscious Mind To Get What You Want. Retrieved March 5, 2020, from https://www.forbes.com/sites/briannawiest/2018/09/12/13-ways-to-start-training-your-subconscious-mind-to-get-what-you-want/#60f32fd37d69

Young, H. (2020, January 22). 5 Little Known Tips To Harness Subconscious Mind Healing Power. Retrieved March 12, 2020, from https://subconsciousservant.com/subconscious-mind-healing-power/